MOTHER SONGS

MOTHER SONGS

Poems
for, by, and about
Mothers

EDITED BY
SANDRA M. GILBERT,
SUSAN GUBAR,
AND DIANA O'HEHIR

W. W. Norton & Company

NEW YORK   LONDON

The text of this book is composed in Centaur with the display
set in Centaur with Caslon Swash Capitals
Composition and manufacturing by the Haddon Craftsmen Inc.
Book design by Charlotte Staub

Library of Congress Cataloging-in-Publication Data

Mothersongs : poems for, by, and about mothers / edited by Sandra
M. Gilbert, Susan Gubar, and Diana O'Hehir.

    p.   cm.
    Includes index.
    1. Mothers—Poetry. 2. Motherhood—Poetry. 3. Mother
and child—Poetry. 4. American poetry. 5. English poetry.
I. Gilbert, Sandra M. II. Gubar, Susan, 1944– . III. O'Hehir,
Diana, 1929– .
PS595.M64M697   1995
811.008'03520431—dc20   94-42757
ISBN 0-393-03771-1

W. W. Norton & Company, Inc.
500 Fifth Avenue,
New York, N.Y. 10110
W. W. Norton & Company Ltd.
10 Coptic Street,
London WCIA IPU

1 2 3 4 5 6 7 8 9 0

Contents

II
Love's Labor:
Birthing and Nursing

III
Mother Talk:
Living with Children

IV
THE LOST CHILD:
MOTHER GRIEF

V

IN THE FLOOD OF REMEMBRANCE: STORIES ABOUT OUR MOTHERS

VI
A WOMAN *Is* HER MOTHER:
MY MOTHER/MY SELF

VII
TO MY FIRST LOVE:
CELEBRATING THE MOTHER

VIII
SILVER THREADS:
THE AGING MOTHER

IX
MY GRANDMOTHERS WERE STRONG: EXPLORING ORIGINS

X
AFTER MY MOTHER DIED:
PRAYERS AND FAREWELLS

XI

THE MOTHER OF US ALL:
MYTHS OF MATERNITY

XII

CONCEIVING THE MOTHER: MEANINGS OF MATERNITY

Preface

🌿

$\mathcal{T}$he first songs we hear are mothers' songs—lullabies and nursery rhymes teaching us about the world, the self, and language. For almost everyone, as the American poet H.D. once mused, "the first deity . . . the first love" is "Maia, mama, Mutter, mut, mamalie, mimmie, Madre, Mary, *mother*." Yet this book of *MotherSongs* represents a striking change in our society. Although maternity has been celebrated and consecrated for centuries, and although as primary caretakers mothers have always helped shape civilization, poets have just in the last few decades begun to speak *as* mothers and *about* mothers with unprecedented complexity, intensity, and subtlety.

Of course, the great artists of the English language have written often, and passionately, about mythic mothers, mother goddesses, and nurturing muses. In the fourteenth century, the medieval mystic Julian of Norwich proclaimed that "nature, love, wisdom and knowledge" are "the property of motherhood," expressing the same awe of maternal power that inspired a range of writers to evoke or examine, among other figures, the classical deities Demeter and Urania as well as the biblical personages Eve and Mary. Few major poets of the past, however, meditated at any length on the meaning of maternity, and still fewer focused in verse on their own particular mothers.

In fact, it was not until the nineteenth century, with its sanctification of motherhood, that maternity became a popular literary topic, especially among some women poets and readers. Perhaps, though, because the subject was so often sentimentalized, serious writers rarely turned to it. Such men of letters as Charles Dickens and Mark Twain scoffed at the emotional excesses they associated with versified mother love, while aesthetically ambitious women like George Eliot and Emily Dickinson tended to shrink from the mawkishness they connected with a contaminated tradition. To many thinkers, the words "mother" and "poet" seemed to be contradictory terms: the Victorian ideology of maternity defined a mother as a selfless creature who lived entirely for her children while it was thought that a true poet had to have what the age saw as "masculine" qualities of authority and assertiveness.

The situation changed, and changed radically, in the twentieth century. Once women gained legal, political, social, economic, and intellectual rights that they had never been able to claim before, creativity and procreativity no longer appeared contradictory. Beginning especially with the generation that came of age in the fifties and sixties, women poets have combined literary creativity with biological procreativity, often using their art to describe their own physical and metaphysical experiences of motherhood. Clearly many feel, with the writer Robin Morgan, that "it is refreshing at last to be able to come out of my mother-closet and yell to the world that I love my dear wonderful delicious child."

What intensifies this impulse to "come out" as a mother and examine in public the private pleasures or pains of family life is the fascination with personal detail, with what we might call the extraordinary resonance of the apparently ordinary, that has characterized poetry in English for the last four or five decades. In the years since World War II, both the "beats" (represented by, say, Allen Ginsberg) and the "confessional" poets (including, most prominently, Robert Lowell, Sylvia Plath, and Anne Sexton) began to mine a rich vein of vivid particularity as they turned memories, dreams, and wishes into art. Inevitably, then, both men and women remembered mama in poetry, often addressing the mother directly to praise or blame her ways, question or quarrel with her influence, eulogize or elegize her life.

This new and unprecedented outpouring of mother songs means that a disproportionate number of our selections here were written quite recently. More than half of our poets are still alive and well; many are bringing up children even as they write about bringing up children. Nevertheless, we have also incorporated a group of strong, historically fascinating works into our collection: medieval ballads, courtly lyrics, Romantic musings, Victorian meditations.

Who are our poets? Vital and diverse, they speak for

and about a host of traditions in both motherhood and poetry even while they write in many different modes and manners. Among earlier artists, some are elegantly witty seventeenth-century metaphysicals (John Donne, Richard Crashaw); some are suave cavaliers (Robert Herrick, Ambrose Philips); some are allegedly "blue-stocking" women intellectuals (Anne Bradstreet, Katherine Philips); and others are Romantic or post-Romantic celebrants of the nature of the maternal and the maternal in nature (William Wordsworth, John Keats, Walt Whitman). Among twentieth-century poets, the book represents such pioneers of modernism as D. H. Lawrence, Marianne Moore, Wallace Stevens, and William Carlos Williams. And among our contemporaries, the writers collected here include African-American memoirists (Lucille Clifton, Colleen McElroy, Yusef Komunyakaa), feminist poet-novelists (Erica Jong, Alice Walker), and lesbian visionaries (Marilyn Hacker, Audre Lorde), along with such well-known recent mythologists of the family as Robert Lowell, Sylvia Plath, Anne Sexton, and Sharon Olds.

Diverse as their backgrounds are, all these poets share H.D.'s sense that the first deity, the first love, is "Maia, mama." To emphasize both the variety and the commonality of maternal experience, we have organized our anthology around twelve crucial aspects of motherhood, each approached from a number of different positions. Poems about pregnancy, labor, delivery, and nursing begin the book, taking up Parts I ("With Child") and II ("Love's Labor"), and here a majority of the pieces are written from the point of view of the new mother. The maternal voice still dominates, too, in Parts III ("Mother Talk") and IV ("The Lost Child"), inflecting works that dramatize the experiences of women raising daughters and sons or mourning children lost through miscarriage, abortion, stillbirth, disease, war, slavery, or other causes.

Section V of *MotherSongs* ("In the Flood of Remembrance") offers a different perspective on maternity: Here the mother is addressed or recalled by sons and daughters exploring the memories and meanings she symbolizes for her children. In a similar vein, the question of inheritance—of what the maternal bequeaths—shapes many of the poems that follow. Part VI ("A Woman *Is* Her Mother") includes poems examining the phenomenon that the sociologist Nancy Chodorow calls "fluid boundaries"—the close relationship between certain mothers and daughters that sometimes seems even to blur the separate identity of each. Part VII ("To My First Love") focuses on celebrations of maternal power while Parts VIII and IX ("Silver Threads" and "My Grandmothers Were Strong") bring together analyses of aging mothers and tributes to the greatness, even grandeur, of grandmothers, some intimately connected with the speakers and some imaginatively reinvented.

The last three sections of *MotherSongs* contain some of the most ambitious texts in the volume. Part X ("After My Mother Died") offers formal and informal elegies for lost mothers while Part XI ("The Mother of Us All") includes meditations on madonnas, muses, and mother goddesses who represent a number of different traditions. Finally, Part XII ("Conceiving the Mother") reveals the complicated strategies poets have used to analyze the many meanings of maternity: some writers have focused on metaphors for the mother and the mother as metaphor; others have considered the politics of parenting; still others have brooded on the human implications of animal motherhood; and quite a few have theorized the moral trials and triumphs of particular historical mothers.

It is our hope that, from Plath's "Morning Song" about nursing a newborn baby to the mourning songs of writers lamenting their own lost mothers, *MotherSongs* will document the vitality of new traditions in our literature and our lives. Sharon Olds's "Language of the Brag" succinctly summarizes the aesthetic of maternal pride that inspires so many of the mother poems we have collected here. Wanting "some epic use for my excellent body," the poet boasts that "this giving birth, this glistening verb" can stand beside the achievements of such men as Walt Whitman and Allen Ginsberg. Her tone is comic but her point is deeply serious. Taken together, all the writers represented in this anthology—American and British, female and male, Jewish and Christian, African-American and Chicano—bear witness to the many ways in which the powers, pains, and pleasures of maternity can be transformed into powerful art.

In exploring this art and assembling this anthology, we have been supported and counseled by a number of people. We are grateful to Ellen Levine for her encouragement of the project and to Jill Bialosky for her continuing warmth, sustenance, and attention. For research and clerical assistance, we want to thank John Beckman, Lisa Harper and—especially, for last-minute aid—Chris Sindt, while for significant orientation and scholarship in this field we are extremely grateful to Paula Harrington, and for much lively advice as well as for many invaluable contributions we are deeply indebted to Susanna Gilbert.

I

WITH CHILD: THE MOTHER-TO-BE

*W*hen is *one* also *two*? How can the self enclose an other? What blood relative is necessarily a mysterious stranger? These puzzling questions touch on a few of the paradoxes of pregnancy, an adventure that for many of the poets represented here is as metaphysical as it is physical. Indeed, both Sylvia Plath's "You're" and Anne Waldman's "Enceinte" dramatize maternal expectations through riddles. The unknown child inside her body is "vague as fog and looked for like mail," muses Plath, and Waldman breathlessly lists a series of alternative metaphors for the conundrum that inhabits her: her baby is "a cushion, veiled lamp, some-kind-of-moveable-parts-doll-deity, sponge, rising loaf, butterfly, trapped bird." Perhaps, the words of these writers suggest, the mother-to-be experiences in her own flesh the closest possible encounter with the mystery of the future, the enigma of the new. "We are about to become!" exults Kathleen Fraser while Erica Jong celebrates "ten toes, ten fingers/& infinite hope." Pregnancy, announces Barbara Ras, is "a state of mind so full/nothing else can be," and in this state "Our talk slows to the lengthening loop of the blood,/pauses for tiny hands, tiny feet to beat their sayso."

With Child

Now I am slow and placid, fond of sun,
Like a sleek beast, or a worn one:
No slim and languid girl—not glad
With the windy trip I once had,
But velvet-footed, musing of my own,
Torpid, mellow, stupid as a stone.

You cleft me with your beauty's pulse, and now
Your pulse has taken body. Care not how
The old grace goes, how heavy I am grown,
Big with this loneliness, how you alone
Ponder our love. Touch my feet and feel
How earth tingles, teeming at my heel!
Earth's urge, not mine—my little death, not hers;
And the pure beauty yearns and stirs.
It does not heed our ecstasies, it turns
With secrets of its own, its own concerns,
Toward a windy world of its own, toward stark
And solitary places. In the dark,
Defiant even now, it tugs and moans
To be untangled from these mother's bones.

GENEVIEVE TAGGARD

Poems for the New

1.

we're connecting,
    foot under my rib.
I'm sore with life!
At night,

    your toes grow. Inches of the new!
The lion prowls the sky
and shakes his tail for you.
Pieces of moon
        fly by my kitchen window.
And your father comes
riding the lions back
        in the dark,
to hold me,
        you,
            in the perfect circle of him.

2.

Voluptuous against him, I am
nothing superfluous,
but all—
bones, bark of him, root of him take.
I am round
with his sprouting,
new thing new thing!

He wraps me.
The sheets are white.
My belly has tracks on it—
                    hands and feet
are moving
under this taut skin.
In snow, in light,
we are about to become!

KATHLEEN FRASER

The Buddha in the Womb

Bobbing in the waters of the womb,
little godhead, ten toes, ten fingers
& infinite hope,
sails upside down through the world.

My bones, I know, are only a cage
for death.
Meditating, I can see my skull,
a death's head,
lit from within
by candles
which are possibly the suns
of other galaxies.

I know that death
is a movement toward light,
a happy dream
from which you are loath to awaken,
a lover left
in a country
to which you have no visa,
& I know that the horses of the spirit
are galloping, galloping, galloping
out of time
& into the moment called NOW.

Why then do I care
for this upside-down Buddha
bobbling through the world,
his toes, his fingers
alive with blood
that will only sing & die?

There is a light in my skull
& a light in his.
We meditate on our bones only
to let them blow away
with fewer regrets.

Flesh is merely a lesson.
We learn it
& pass on.

ERICA JONG

Pregnancy

It is the best thing.
I should always like to be pregnant,

Tummy thickening like a yoghurt,
Unbelievable flower.

A queen is always pregnant with her country.
Sheba of questions

Or briny siren
At her difficult passage,

One is the mountain that moves
Toward the earliest gods.

Who started this?
An axis, a quake, a perimeter,

I have no decisions to master
That could change my frame

Or honor.
Immaculate. Or if it was not, perfect.

Pregnant, I'm highly explosive—
You can feel it, long before

Your seed will run back to hug you—
Squaring and cubing

Into reckless bones, bouncing odd ways
Like a football.

The heart sloshes through the microphone
Like falls in a box canyon.

The queen's only a figurehead.
Nine months pulled by nine

Planets, the moon sloping
Through its amnion sea,

Trapped, stone-mad . . . and three
Beings' lives gel in my womb.

SANDRA MCPHERSON

You're

Clownlike, happiest on your hands,
Feet to the stars, and moon-skulled,
Gilled like a fish. A common-sense
Thumbs-down on the dodo's mode.
Wrapped up in yourself like a spool,
Trawling your dark as owls do.
Mute as a turnip from the Fourth
Of July to All Fools' Day,
O high-riser, my little loaf.

Vague as fog and looked for like mail.
Farther off than Australia.
Bent-backed Atlas, our traveled prawn.

Snug as a bud and at home
Like a sprat in a pickle jug.
A creel of eels, all ripples.
Jumpy as a Mexican bean.
Right, like a well-done sum.
A clean slate, with your own face on.

SYLVIA PLATH

Enceinte

Mossy rock, tree limb, foot of a rabbit, large edible root, serpent lashing from side to side, a cushion, veiled lamp, some-kind-of moveable-parts-doll-deity, sponge, rising loaf, butterfly, trapped bird, wax, mold, flame, a small man writing, small woman eating & lifting elbow, a bat, succulent plant, something in the oven, a potato doll, a doll of seashells, sandbag, large fish swimming in circles, a clock, something silent, a silent toy car, a memory, coiled & striking, fish hidden behind rock, every color & no color, a telephone receiver, submarine, rubber expanding, held together with rubber bands, labial, fingers playing an instrument, inflatable doll, a school of dolphins, tidal wave, unease, planet with circling rings, not made in a lab, a thunder storm, lashing out, a chest of toys, sedentary monkey, jack-in-a-box, icebox, lamps going on, a solar system, a tiny city ruled by a cobra, a city of clam inhabitants, an excursion, a place with hats on, an owl, a bear in a cave, drifting raft, boat on the waves, electricity, dancing flame's shadow on your face, bulging package, a rushed person gesturing excitedly as in hailing a speeding taxi cab, quicksilver.

ANNE WALDMAN

The Stethoscope

Like Halley's comet, bending on its tail,
you curl beneath the black cup on my skin:
I guess at limbs in half-eclipse, obscure
and fluent as a distant telegram.
Unworldly, small, sealed orders, darkroom heat,
soon among the signals pulsed, the static whoosh,
    arrives
in distant thuds your rapider than human
heartbeat—sex unknowable—bud eyes—

Yet of our world you only know the tree
you lie beneath, its root your belly, fronds
and villi falling in the sunken lake
of capillaries, bubbles, breathing bonds . . .
I sigh. And somewhere you incline your vast
night-sighted brow—your jointed, swimming hands—

ANNE WINTERS

A Timepiece

Of a pendulum's mildness, with her feet up
My sister lay expecting her third child.
Over the hammock's crescent spilled
Her flushed face, grazing clover and buttercup.

Her legs were troubling her, a vein had burst.
Even so, among partial fullnesses she lay
Of pecked damson, of daughters at play
Who in the shadow of the house rehearsed

Her gait, her gesture, unnatural to them,
But they would master it soon enough, grown tall
Trusting that out of themselves came all
That full grace, while she out of whom these came

Shall have thrust fullness from her, like a death.
Already, seeing the little girls listless
She righted herself in a new awkwardness.
It was not *her* life she was heavy with.

Let us each have some milk, my sister smiled
Meaning to muffle with the taste
Of unbuilt bone a striking in her breast,
For soon by what it tells the clock is stilled.

JAMES MERRILL

Before the Birth of One of Her Children

All things within this fading world hath end,
Adversity doth still our joys attend;
No ties so strong, no friends so dear and sweet
But with death's parting blow is sure to meet.
The sentence past is most irrevocable,
A common thing, yet oh, inevitable.
How soon, my Dear, death may my steps attend,
How soon't may be thy lot to lose thy friend,
We both are ignorant, yet love bids me
These farewell lines to recommend to thee,
That when that knot's untied that made us one,
I may seem thine, who in effect am none.
And if I see not half my days that's due,
What nature would, God grant to yours and you;
The many faults that well you know I have
Let be interred in my oblivious grave;
If any worth or virtue were in me,
Let that live freshly in thy memory
And when thou feel'st no grief, as I no harms,
Yet love thy dead, who long lay in thine arms.
And when thy loss shall be repaid with gains
Look to my little babes, my dear remains.
And if thou love thyself, or loved'st me,
These O protect from step-dame's injury.
And if chance to thine eyes shall bring this verse,
With some sad sighs honour my absent hearse;

And kiss this paper for thy love's dear sake,
Who with salt tears this last farewell did take.

ANNE BRADSTREET

The Expectant Father

The skin of my mouth, chewed raw, tastes good.
I get up, cursing, and find the bottle of Scotch.
My mouth burns as darkness, lifting her skirt,
reveals daylight, a sleek left ankle.
The woman calls. I don't answer.
I imagine myself coming up to my own door,
holding a small reed basket in my arms.
Inside it, there is a child,
with clay tablets instead of hands,
and my name is written on each one.
The woman calls me again and I go to her.
She reaches for me, but I move away.
I frown, pulling back the covers to look at her.
So much going on outside;
the walls could cave in on us any time, any time.
I bring my face down
where the child's head should be and press hard.
I feel pain, she's pulling my hair.
I rise up, finally, and back away from the bed,
while she turns on her side
and drags her legs up to her chest.

I wait for her to cry,
then go into the kitchen.
I fix a Scotch and sit down at the table.
In six months, it is coming, in six months,
and I have no weapon against it.

Aɪ

Weathering Out

She liked mornings the best—Thomas gone
to look for work, her coffee flushed with milk,

outside autumn trees blowsy and dripping.
Past the seventh month she couldn't see her feet

so she floated from room to room, houseshoes flapping,
navigating corners in wonder. When she leaned

against a door jamb to yawn, she disappeared entirely.

Last week they had taken a bus at dawn
to the new airdock. The hangar slid open in segments

and the zeppelin nosed forward in its silver envelope.
The men walked it out gingerly, like a poodle,

then tied it to a mast and went back inside.
Beulah felt just that large and placid, a lake;

she glistened from cocoa butter smoothed in
when Thomas returned every evening nearly

in tears. He'd lean an ear on her belly
and say: *Little fellow's really talking,*

though to her it was more the *pok-pok-pok*
of a fingernail tapping a thick cream lampshade.

Sometimes during the night she woke and found him
asleep there and the child sleeping, too.

The coffee was good but too little. Outside
everything shivered in tinfoil—only the clover

between the cobblestones hung stubbornly on,
green as an afterthought. . . .

RITA DOVE

Letter in July

My life slows and deepens.
I am thirty-eight, neither here nor there.
It is a morning in July, hot and clear.
Out in the field, a bird repeats its quaternary call,
four notes insisting, *I'm here, I'm here.*
The field is unmowed, summer's wreckage everywhere.
Even this early, all is expectancy.

It is as if I float on a still pond,
drowsing in the bottom of a rowboat,
curled like a leaf into myself.

The water laps at its old wooden sides
as the sun beats down on my body,
a wand, an enchantment, shaping it
into something languid and new.

A year ago, two, I dreamed I held
a mirror to your unborn face and saw you,
in that warped, watery glass, not as a child
but as you will be twenty years from now.
I woke, a light breeze lifting the curtain,
as if touched by a ghost's thin hand,
light filling the room, coming from nowhere.

I know the time, the place of our meeting.
It will be January, the coldest night
of the year. You will be carrying a lantern
as you enter the world crying,
and I cry to hear you cry.
A moment that, even now,
I carry in my body.

ELIZABETH SPIRES

Pregnant Poets Swim Lake Tarleton, New Hampshire

For Emily Wheeler

You dive in, head for the other side, sure
that to swim a lake means to cross it,

whole. I am slow to follow,
repelled by edgewater rife with growth, the darker
suck of the deep. You lead,
letting go so surely you possess. I surrender.
Midlake we rest, breathless, let up our feet.
Our bellies are eight-month fruits
fabulous with weightlessness.
We have entered summer like a state of pasture,
pregnancy like a state of mind so full
nothing else can be.
Sharing this is simple: the surprise of a tomato
still perfect after days in a pocket.
Brown lines began in pubic hair, arced
up abdomens to our navels.
Here is the circle made flesh.
How much water does it take to make blood?
Where do Tibetans get the conches
they blow to release the trapped sound of the sea?
Our talk slows to the lengthening loop of the blood,
pauses for tiny hands, tiny feet to beat their sayso.
"Marianne" lasts as long as a complete sentence
before the next utterance floats up, "Moore."
We are the gardens. We are the toads.
The season of wetness is upon us.
Leap. Leap for all the kingdoms
and all the waters,
the water that breaks,
the rain, the juice, the tide,
the dark water that draws light down to life.

BARBARA RAS

II

$\mathcal{L}$OVE'S LABOR:
BIRTHING AND
NURSING

$\mathcal{T}$he paradoxes of childbirth—its fierce pains
and pleasures—are related to the mystery of how one
being becomes definitively two. An involuntary physical
act that has nevertheless been imagined as a miraculous
spiritual revelation, delivery produces an infant who may
seem, on the one hand, like the most vulnerable of ani-
mals and, on the other, like the wisest of emissaries. The
poems in this section explore the points of view of many
different participants in childbirth and nursing scenes:
teenage mothers, new fathers, even the suckling infant.
Some of the works are poignantly funny: in the grip of
powerful contractions, Linda Pastan's laboring speaker

comes to believe that "babies should grow in fields" so they could be "picked" like beets or turnips. Some are sad: the baby of William Blake's "Infant Song" struggles against parental care that feels confining, even oddly enervating.

Yet in their various ways, all the works here deal with the surprising and often inexplicable separateness of the newborn child as well as the feelings of protectiveness, anxiety, and wonder the infant evokes. As the tranquil mother in Anne Winters's sonnet sequence "Elizabeth Near and Far" muses to her baby, "There is space between me, I know,/and you" and that space—in which the mother becomes the child's first other, turning them each into an individual sphere or world—is bridged by her intense emotional attachment, the maternal bond: "One planet loves the other."

Notes from the Delivery Room

Strapped down,
victim in an old comic book,
I have been here before,
this place where pain winces
off the walls
like too bright light.
Bear down a doctor says,
foreman to sweating laborer,
but this work, this forcing
of one life from another
is something that I signed for
at a moment when I would have signed anything.
Babies should grow in fields;
common as beets or turnips
they should be picked and held
root end up, soil spilling
from between their toes—
and how much easier it would be later,
returning them to earth.
Bear up . . . bear down . . . the audience
grows restive, and I'm a new magician
who can't produce the rabbit
from my swollen hat.
She's crowning, someone says,
but there is no one royal here,
just me, quite barefoot,
greeting my barefoot child.

LINDA PASTAN

45

Sounding

Annie Cameron

Four months in the womb
you were photographed
with sound. We stared

at the pulsing surface
of your skull, your fingers
lifting, as if to stave off

a sudden wind in that
sealed room where for
so long only our two

hearts echoed each other.
Screened, your heart glowed
at the joint of the caliper.

Months later, after
they had bathed you
and brought you to me,

I washed you again—
in privacy, opened
one by one the clenched

fingers seen too soon,
brushed the thin skin
of the skull where

the brain's leaping blood
bulged against it.
For months, I'd heard it

46

in dreams: the underwater gong
then the regular shock waves—
an assault as barbaric as conception,

the soul rung forward into image,
as metal is stunned into coin,
as the hammer sounds against its resistance:

the gold unblinking eye of the forge.

CAROL MUSKE

Loba in Childbed

She lay in bed, screaming, the boat
carried her to the heart of the mandala
sweat stuck
hair to her forehead, she
lay back, panting, remembering
it was what she *should* do. Skull boat
carried her to the heart of her womb, red
pulsing eye of her spirit. She saw
soul shine shoaled on rocks, flint edges
of rocky pelvic cage, caught, swirls
of bland liquid eddying round
curls of bright
red-gold hair, she
screamed, for him, for herself, she
tried to open, to widen tunnel, the rock
inside her tried to crack, to chip away

bright spirit hammered at it w/ his
soft foamy head
                    she cried out
bursting from the heart
                            of the devastated
mandala, skull boat grew wings
                                she fluttered
thru amniotic seas to draw him on.

            Gold
            swirling sun, gold
            swirling folds of
            kesa, enfolding, blinding
            her opaquer eyes
            the speck
            of red alchemic gold
            caught in black
            womb spasm
            struggled weaker
            toward earthlight
            she offered.

It was
round stone head monolith
lying in Colombian jungle
tried to articulate, to burst
out of her.

It was
line drawing bird soul

as in hieroglyphs or in
Indian drawing fluttered
down to meet her

Snatches of brief music, unremitting
white pain, his only
signals.

———◆———

Dark cave. Dark forces countering
magic w/ magic. No time
to navigate now; no white
quartz, no lapis, incense, blessed
flowery water. Only
shrill mantra scream, arch
mudra of tossing pain
torture of watching spirit, measured
in pulse beat   from wires tied
to heart of her cunt, center
of her womb. Have the oceanic
presences deserted her?

> She walked moaning
> into dry heart of
> sandstone continent
> snatched pale
> phosphorescing son
> from red cliffs,
> the sun
> flashed like pain
> behind her eyes

———◆———

Was he limp, did he stir
w/ life, did she hear
his soft breath in her ear?

DIANE DI PRIMA

The Loba Sings to Her Cub

O my mole, sudden & perfect
golden gopher tunneling
to light, o separate(d)
strands of our breath!
                              Bright silver
threads of spirit
                    O quicksilver
spurt of fist, scansion of
unfocussed eyeball,
                         grace of yr
cry, or song, my
cry or
        you lie warm,   wet on the
soggy pelt of my
                  hollowed
belly, my
            bones curve up
to embrace you.

DIANE DI PRIMA

Fifteen

I was pregnant that year,
stitching lace and purple-flowered ribbon
to tiny kimonos and sacques.
I still thought sperm
came out like pollen dust in puffs of air.

I ate cream of wheat for breakfast, unsalted,
diapered a rubber doll
in my Red Cross baby care class, and sold
lipsticks and gummy lotions to housewives
to pay for a crib.

Oh, it was something, giving birth.
When my water bag splattered
I screamed, and the neat green anaesthesiologist
said, "Why don't you shut up?"
"Fuck you!" I shrieked.

"Breathe deep," was the last thing
I heard him say.
Ten minutes later I woke up.
The obstetrician with his needle and thread,
busy as a seamstress,

winked at the pink-haired nurse
who brought me my baby girl,
wrinkled and howling.

"She's lovely. I'd like a cheeseburger
and milkshake now," I said.

LUCILLE DAY

From Vision and Prayer

Who
Are you
Who is born
In the next room
So loud to my own
That I can hear the womb
Opening and the dark run
Over the ghost and the dropped son
Behind the wall thin as a wren's bone?
In the birth bloody room unknown
To the burn and turn of time
And the heart print of man
Bows no baptism
But dark alone
Blessing on
The wild
Child.

                               I
                            Must lie
                          Still as stone
                         By the wren bone
                        Wall hearing the moan
                       Of the mother hidden
                      And the shadowed head of pain
                     Casting to-morrow like a thorn
                    And the midwives of miracle sing
                     Until the turbulent new born
                      Burns me his name and his flame
                       And the winged wall is torn
                         By his torrid crown
                          And the dark thrown
                            From his loin
                              To bright
                               Light.

                                        DYLAN THOMAS

Hello

Hel*lo* there, Biscuit! You're a better-looking broad
By much than, and your sister's dancing up & down.
"I just gave one mighty Push"
your mother says, and we are all in business.

                              53

I thought your mother might powder my knuckles
gript at one point, with wild eyes on my tie
"Don't move!" and then the screams began,
they wheeled her off, and we are all in business.

I wish I knew what business (son) we're in
I can't wait seven weeks to see her grin
I'm not myself, we are all changing here
direction *and* velocity, to accommodate you, dear.

JOHN BERRYMAN

From *A Birthday Suite*

For Eve

The Cambridge Afternoon Was Grey

When you were born, the nurse's aide
Wore a grey uniform, and the Evelyn Nursing Home
Was full of Sisters of Mercy starched

To a religious ecstasy
Of tidiness. They brought you, struggling feebly
Inside your cotton blanket, only your eyes

Were looking as if you already knew
What thinking would be like—
Some pinch of thought was making your eyes brim

With diabolic relish, like a child
Who has been hiding crouched down in a closet
Among the woolen overcoats and stacked

Shoeboxes, while the anxious parents
Call *Where are you?* And suddenly the child
Bounces into the room

Pretending innocence. . . . My hot breast
Was delighted, and ran up to you like a dog
To a younger dog it wants to make friends with,

So the scandalized aide had to pull the grey
Curtains around our bed, making a sound
Of hissing virtue, curtainrings on rod,

While your eyes were saying *Where am I? I'm here!*

ALICIA OSTRIKER

Infant Sorrow

My mother groand! my father wept.
Into the dangerous world I leapt:
Helpless, naked, piping loud:
Like a fiend hid in a cloud.

Struggling in my father's hands:
Striving against my swadling bands:

55

Bound and weary I thought best
To sulk upon my mother's breast.

WILLIAM BLAKE

Infant

The head tilts back, like a heavy leaf, the eyes sew shut
With a row of grains, the hand wavers under the chin,
      fingers
Splayed; this is
Exactly the way I remember it;
No syllable different; navy-blue
Boiled eyes, and cuckoo-mouth, cuckoo
Child; all of us always have known,
Recognition printed on the cells
Of the primitive body chart.

Every night that month I dreamed the baby was born,
It was fragile, creased like an overseas envelope; it was
      mislaid;
I had forgotten to feed it.
I woke up, moved my awkward belly into the
      bathroom,
Stood gasping at the edge of the washbasin. I would
      never
Be used to this.

And when I picked up the real baby it settled its
        heavy weight between my arm and my body.
Like a sullen beanbag,
Turned its face against me,
Pulled me into it.

DIANA O'HEHIR

From *The Two-Part Prelude*

                    Blessed the infant babe—
For my best conjectures I would trace
The progress of our being—blest the babe
Nursed in his mother's arms, the babe who sleeps
Upon his mother's breast, who, when his soul
Claims manifest kindred with an earthly soul,
Doth gather passion from his mother's eye.
Such feelings pass into his torpid life
Like an awakening breeze, and hence his mind,
Even in the first trial of its powers,
Is prompt and watchful, eager to combine
In one appearance all the elements
And parts of the same object, else detached
And loth to coalesce. Thus day by day
Subjected to the discipline of love,
His organs and recipient faculties
Are quickened, are more vigorous; his mind spreads,

Tenacious of the forms which it receives.
In one beloved presence—nay and more,
In that most apprehensive habitude
And those sensations which have been derived
From this beloved presence—there exists
A virtue which irradiates and exalts
All objects through all intercourse of sense.
No outcast he, bewildered and depressed;
Along his infant veins are interfused
The gravitation and the filial bond
Of Nature that connect him with the world.
Emphatically such a being lives,
An inmate of this *active* universe.
From Nature largely he receives, nor so
Is satisfied, but largely gives again;
For feeling has to him imparted strength,
And—powerful in all sentiments of grief,
Of exultation, fear and joy—his mind.
Even as an agent of the one great mind,
Creates, creator and receiver both,
Working but in alliance with the works
Which it beholds. Such, verily, is the first
Poetic spirit of our human life—
By uniform control of after years
In most abated and suppressed, in some
Through every change of growth or of decay
Preeminent till death.

WILLIAM WORDSWORTH

Morning Song

Love set you going like a fat gold watch.
The midwife slapped your footsoles, and your bald cry
Took its place among the elements.

Our voices echo, magnifying your arrival. New statue.
In a drafty museum, your nakedness
Shadows our safety. We stand round blankly as walls.

I'm no more your mother
Than the cloud that distills a mirror to reflect its own
    slow
Effacement at the wind's hand.

All night your moth-breath
Flickers among the flat pink roses. I wake to listen:
A far sea moves in my ear.

One cry, and I stumble from bed, cow-heavy and floral
In my Victorian nightgown.
Your mouth opens clean as a cat's. The window square

Whitens and swallows its dull stars. And now you try
Your handful of notes;
The clear vowels rise like balloons.

SYLVIA PLATH

Night Light

Only your plastic night light dusts its pink
on the backs and undersides of things; your mother,
head resting on the nightside of one arm,
floats a hand above your cradle
to feel the humid tendril of your breathing.
Outside, the night rocks, murmurs . . . Crouched
in this eggshell light, I feel my heart
slowing, opened to your tiny flame

as if your blue irises mirrored me
as if your smile breathed and warmed
and curled in your face which is only asleep.
There is space between me, I know,
and you. I hang above you like a planet—
you're a planet, too. One planet loves the other.

ANNE WINTERS

The Chair by the Window

Your rhythmic nursing slows. I feel
your smile before I see it: nipple pinched
in corner of mouth, your brimming, short, tuck-
      cornered
smile. I shake my head, my *no* vibrates

to you through ribs and arms. Your tapered ears
quiver, work faintly and still pinker, my
nipple spins right out and we
are two who sit and smile into each other's eyes.

Again, you frowning farmer, me your cow:
you flap one steadying palm against my breast,
thump down the other, chuckle, snort, and then
you're suddenly under, mouth moving steadily, eyes
drifting past mine abstracted, your familiar
blue remote and window-paned with light.

ANNE WINTERS

Elizabeth Near and Far

You are awake, held in arms, chin
balanced on my shoulder, small globe turning back
while mine much larger faces straight ahead.
It sounds as if you'd found your thumb—you thrum
inward, but audible: *frrum, frrum,* you're talking.
I sense your eyes go past me and around
your thumb to where some floating speck of light
hovers, microscopic, in your glistening gaze.

Or mornings when you lie awake, your first
faint vowels floating up (the nursery door ajar).

You place your hands on air; push, croon, turn,
all softly, all alone (my head half-in the door)
and stroke the wall and murmur in the still-
shaded room, and are alone with yourself.

ANNE WINTERS

The New Toy

She cannot leave it alone,
    The new toy;
She pats it, smooths it, rights it, to show it's her own,
As the other train-passengers muse on its temper and
      tone,
    Till she draws from it cries of annoy: —

She feigns to appear as if thinking it nothing so rare
    Or worthy of pride, to achieve
This wonder a child, though with reason the rest of
      them there
    May so be inclined to believe.

THOMAS HARDY

Black Baby

The baby I hold in my arms is a black baby.
   Today I set him in the sun and
   Sunbeams danced on his head.
The baby I hold in my arms is a black baby.
   I toil, and I cannot always cuddle him.
   I place him on the ground at my feet.
   He presses the warm earth with his hands,
   He lifts the sand and laughs to see
   It flow through his chubby fingers.
   I watch to discern which are his hands,
   Which is the sand. . . .
Lo . . . the rich loam is black like his hands.

The baby I hold in my arms is a black baby.
   Today the coal-man brought me coal.
   Sixteen dollars a ton is the price I pay for coal.—
   Costly fuel . . . though they say:—
   Men must sweat and toil to dig it from the ground.
   Costly fuel . . . 'Tis said:—
   If it is buried deep enough and lies hidden long
     enough
   'Twill be no longer coal but diamonds. . . .
   My black baby looks at me.
   His eyes are like coals,
   They shine like diamonds.

ANITA SCOTT COLEMAN

A Cradle Song

Sweet dreams form a shade,
O'er my lovely infant's head.
Sweet dreams of pleasant streams,
By happy silent moony beams.

Sweet sleep with soft down,
Weave thy brows an infant crown.
Sweet sleep Angel mild,
Hover o'er my happy child.

Sweet smiles in the night,
Hover over my delight.
Sweet smiles, Mother's smiles,
All the livelong night beguiles.

Sweet moans, dovelike sighs,
Chase not slumber from thy eyes.
Sweet moans, sweeter smiles,
All the dovelike moans beguiles.

Sleep sleep happy child.
All creation slept and smil'd.
Sleep sleep, happy sleep,
While o'er thee thy mother weep.

Sweet babe in thy face,
Holy image I can trace.
Sweet babe once like thee,
Thy maker lay and wept for me,

Wept for me, for thee, for all,
When he was an infant small.
Thou his image ever see,
Heavenly face that smiles on thee;

Smiles on thee, on me, on all,
Who become an infant small,
Infant smiles are his own smiles,
Heaven & earth to peace beguiles.

WILLIAM BLAKE

Night Feeding

Deeper than sleep but not so deep as death
I lay there sleeping and my magic head
remembered and forgot.   On first cry I
remembered and forgot and did believe.
I knew love and I knew evil:
woke to the burning song and the tree burning blind,
despair of our days and the calm milk-giver who
knows sleep, knows growth, the sex of fire and grass,
and the black snake with gold bones.

Black sleeps, gold burns;   on second cry I woke
fully and gave to feed and fed on feeding.
Gold seed, green pain, my wizards in the earth
walked through the house, black in the morning dark.
Shadows grew in my veins, my bright belief,

my head of dreams deeper than night and sleep.
Voices of all black animals crying to drink,
cries of all birth arise, simple as we,
found in the leaves, in clouds and dark, in dream,
deep as this hour, ready again to sleep.

MURIEL RUKEYSER

Night Feed

This is dawn.
Believe me
This is your season, little daughter.
The moment daisies open,
The hour mercurial rainwater
Makes a mirror for sparrows.
It's time we drowned our sorrows.

I tiptoe in.
I lift you up
Wriggling
In your rosy, zipped sleeper.
Yes, this is the hour
For the early bird and me
When finder is keeper.

I crook the bottle.
How you suckle!

This is the best I can be,
Housewife
To this nursery
Where you hold on,
Dear Life.

A silt of milk.
The last suck.
And now your eyes are open,
Birth-colored and offended.
Earth wakes.
You go back to sleep.
The feed is ended.

Worms turn.
Stars go in.
Even the moon is losing face.
Poplars stilt for dawn
And we begin
The long fall from grace.
I tuck you in.

EAVAN BOLAND

Eating Babies

1

Fat
Is the soul of this flesh.
Eat with your hands, slow, you will understand
breasts, why everyone
adores them—Rubens' great custard nudes—why
we can't help sleeping with
pillows.

The old woman in the park pointed,
Is it yours?
Her gold eye-teeth gleamed.

I bend down, taste the fluted
nipples, the elbows, the pads
of the feet. Nibble earlobes, dip
my tongue in the salt fold
of shoulder and throat.

Even now he is changing,
as if I were
licking him thin.

2

He squeezes his eyes tight
to hide
and blink! he's still here.
It's always a surprise.

Safety-fat,
angel-fat,

steal it in mouthfuls,
store it away
where you save

the face that you touched
for the last time
over and over,
your eyes closed

so it wouldn't go away.

3

Watch him sleeping. Touch
the pulse where
the bones haven't locked
in his damp hair:
the navel of dreams.
His eyes open for a moment, underwater.

His arms drift in the dark
as your breath
washes over him.

Bite one cheek. Again.
it's your own
life you lean over, greedy,
going back for more.

CHANA BLOCH

Upon Her Soothing Breast

Upon her soothing breast
She lulled her little child;
A winter sunset in the west,
A dreary glory smiled.

EMILY BRONTË

Nick and the Candlestick

I am a miner. The light burns blue.
Waxy stalactites
Drip and thicken, tears

The earthen womb
Exudes from its dead boredom.
Black bat airs

Wrap me, raggy shawls,
Cold homicides.
They weld to me like plums.

Old cave of calcium
Icicles, old echoer.
Even the newts are white,

Those holy Joes.
And the fish, the fish—
Christ! they are panes of ice,

A vice of knives,
A piranha
Religion, drinking

Its first communion out of my live toes.
The candle
Gulps and recovers its small altitude,

Its yellows hearten.
O love, how did you get here?
O embryo

Remembering, even in sleep,
Your crossed position.
The blood blooms clean

In you, ruby.
The pain
You wake to is not yours.

Love, love,
I have hung our cave with roses,
With soft rugs—

The last of Victoriana.
Let the stars
Plummet to their dark address,

Let the mercuric
Atoms that cripple drip
Into the terrible well,

You are the one
Solid the spaces lean on, envious.
You are the baby in the barn.

SYLVIA PLATH

Unfinished Business

Milk flows, the pact
is made. We hold you
in the crook of an arm,

skin to skin, bare speech
you'll try to recall years
from now.

Daughters, beached on our
shores, there is
unfinished

business between us,
for the sons belong to the fathers
but you

are ours by right
of need, we
whose mothers were sent

away from their homes
unsatisfied,
to live out

the stations of the house,
domestic Calvary,
languishing

for tenderness.
We turn on you and teach
the strictest

art to resuscitate
our care-starved
hearts. We

teach you to mend
holes, rents,
absence;

to tend: to bear
the harness of
unsleeping watchfulness,

pick up our least
pulse of distress;
to cook

and fetch so we,
collapsed with feverish hungers,
can be fed.

Remember, mother,
my frightened child's eyes
staring at you

lying so often, pale,
in bed, I thought
you'd die,

and wondered if
some wrong I'd done
would take you from me.

I ate and ate, to keep us both alive
as now my daughter does
straining to do my bidding.

At the breast there is
the pounding of the heart
bearing

story after story.

CELIA GILBERT

III

MOTHER TALK:
LIVING WITH
CHILDREN

*D*o you expect me always to be responsible for you?" Stevie Smith's apocryphal mother asks in her poem "She said . . ." The mothers who speak in this section variously answer, *yes, I am* responsible for you; responsible with protection, instruction, recognition; responsible with love ranging from the mystic identification of Audre Lorde's "You, flowing through selves/toward You" to the affectionate irony of Ursula Le Guin's "Nothing you do will ever be right/Nothing you do is wrong." The mother has conflicting emotions and so does the child: "I'd fry/her head if I could until/she cried love, love me!" notes Shirley Kaufman.

Finally, Ruth Stone is amusedly self-aware, watching her daughters grow up and suspecting that they are "singing, sprinkle snow down on Mama's hair/And lordy, give us our share."

There are many ways of living with a child, of nurturing, understanding, teaching. The process includes all possible shades and intensities of mother care, concluding with the *grow up and become yourself* implied by Stevie Smith's poetic irony.

Now That I Am Forever with Child

How the days went
while you were blooming within me
I remember   each upon each—
the swelling changed planes of my body

and how you first fluttered   then jumped
and I thought it was my heart.

How the days wound down
and the turning of winter
I recall   you
growing heavy against the wind.
I thought   now her hands
are formed   her hair
has started to curl
now her teeth are done
now she sneezes.

Then the seed opened.
I bore you one morning
just before spring
my head rang like a fiery piston
my legs were towers between which
a new world was passing.

Since then
I can only distinguish

one thread within running hours
you   flowing through selves
toward You.

AUDRE LORDE

Maternity

Maternity is common, but not so
It seemed to me. Motherless, I did not know—
I was all unprepared to feel this glow,
Holy as a Madonna's, and as crude
As any animal's beatitude—
Crude as my own black cat's, who used to bring
Her newest litter to me every spring,
And say, with green eyes shining in the sun:
"Behold this miracle that I have done."

ALICE DUER MILLER

The Gift

Lord, You may not recognize me
speaking for someone else.
I have a son. He is
so little, so ignorant.

He likes to stand
at the screen door, calling
oggie, oggie, entering
language, and sometimes
a dog will stop and come up
the walk, perhaps
accidentally. May he believe
this is not an accident?
At the screen
welcoming each beast
in love's name, Your emissary.

LOUISE GLÜCK

Looking at Them Asleep

When I come home late at night and go in to kiss the
    children,
I see my girl with her arm curled around her head,
her face deep in unconsciousness—so
deeply centered she is in her dark self,
her mouth slightly puffed like one sated but
slightly pouted like one who hasn't had enough,
her eyes so closed you would think they have rolled the
iris around to face the back of her head,
the eyeball marble-naked under that
thick satisfied desiring lid,
she lies on her back in abandon and sealed completion,

and the son in his room, oh the son he is sideways in
     his bed,
one knee up as if he is climbing
sharp stairs up into the night,
and under his thin quivering eyelids you
know his eyes are wide open and
staring and glazed, the blue in them so
anxious and crystally in all this darkness, and his
mouth is open, he is breathing hard from the climb
and panting a bit, his brow is crumpled
and pale, his long fingers curved,
his hand open, and in the center of each hand
the dry dirty boyish palm
resting like a cookie. I look at him in his
quest, the thin muscles of his arms
passionate and tense, I look at her with her
face like the face of a snake who has swallowed a deer,
content, content—and I know if I wake her she'll
smile and turn her face toward me though
half asleep and open her eyes and I
know if I wake him he'll jerk and say Don't and sit
up and stare about him in blue
unrecognition, oh my Lord how I
know these two. When love comes to me and says
What do you know, I say This girl, this boy.

SHARON OLDS

82

Child

Your clear eye is the one absolutely beautiful thing.
I want to fill it with color and ducks,
The zoo of the new

Whose names you meditate—
April snowdrop, Indian pipe,
Little

Stalk without wrinkle,
Pool in which images
Should be grand and classical

Not this troublous
Wringing of hands, this dark
Ceiling without a star.

SYLVIA PLATH

Night-Pieces: For a Child

The Crib

You sleeping I bend to cover.
Your eyelids work. I see
your dream, cloudy as a negative,
swimming underneath.
You blurt a cry. Your eyes

83

spring open, still filmed in dream.
Wider, they fix me—
—death's head, sphinx, medusa?
You scream.
Tears lick my cheeks, my knees
droop at your fear.
Mother I no more am,
but woman, and nightmare.

Her Waking

Tonight I jerk astart in a dark
hourless as Hiroshima,
almost hearing you breathe
in a cot three doors away.

You still breathe, yes—
and my dream with its gift of knives,
its murderous hider and seeker,
ebbs away, recoils

back into the egg of dreams,
the vanishing point of mind.
All gone.

ADRIENNE RICH

She said . . .

She said as she tumbled the baby in:
There, little baby, go sink or swim,
I brought you into the world, what more should I do?
Do you expect me always to be responsible for you?

STEVIE SMITH

To Miss Charlotte Pulteney
in Her Mother's Arms

Timely blossom, infant fair,
Fondling of a happy pair,
Every morn, and every night,
Their solicitous delight,
Sleeping, waking, still at ease,
Pleasing, without skill to please,
Little gossip, blithe and hale,
Tatling many a broken tale,
Singing many a tuneless song,
Lavish of a heedless tongue,
Simple maiden, void of art,
Babbling out the very heart,
Yet abandon'd to thy will,
Yet imagining no ill,
Yet too innocent to blush,
Like the linlet in the bush,

To the Mother-linnet's note
Moduling her slender throat,
Chirping forth thy petty joys,
Wanton in the change of toys,
Like the linnet green, in *May*,
Flitting to each bloomy spray,
Wearied then, and glad of rest,
Like the linlet in the nest.
This thy present happy lot,
This, in time, will be forgot:
Other pleasures, other cares,
Ever-busy Time prepares.
And thou shalt in thy daughter see,
This picture, once, resembled thee.

AMBROSE PHILIPS

Seizure

I gave you what I could when you were born,
salt water to rock you,
your half of nine month's meat,
miles of finished veins,
and all the blood I had to spare.

And then I said, this is the last time
I divide myself in half, the last time
I lie down in danger and rise bereft,
the last time I give up half my blood.

Fifteen months later, when I walked into your room
your mobile of the sun, moon,
and stars was tilting
while your lips twisted,
while you arched your back.

Your fingers groped for something in the air.
Your arms and legs flailed like broken wings.
Your breath was a load too heavy
for your throat to heave into your lungs.
You beat yourself into a daze against your crib.

We slapped your feet,
we flared the lights,
we doused you in a tub of lukewarm water.
But your black eyes rolled.
You had gone somewhere
and left behind a shape of bluish skin,
a counterfeit of you.
                              It was then,
before the red wail of the police car,
before the IV's, before the medicine
dropped into you like angels, before you woke
to a clear brow, to your own funny rising voice,

it was then that I would have struck the bargain,
all my blood
for your small shaking.
I would have called us even.

JEANNE MURRAY WALKER

*An April Fool's Day Present
for My Daughter Elisabeth*

Mother of my granddaughter,
Listen to my song:
A mother can't do right,
A daughter can't be wrong.

I have no claim whatever
On amnesty from you,
Nor will she forgive you
For anything you do.

So are we knit together
By force of opposites,
The daughter that unravels
The skein the mother knits.

One must be divided
So that one be whole,
And this is the duplicity
Alleged of woman's soul.

To be that heavy mother
Who weighs in every thing
Is to be the daughter
Whose footstep is the Spring.

Granddaughter of my mother,
Listen to my song:

Nothing you do will ever be right,
Nothing you do is wrong.

Ursula K. Le Guin

Spelling

My daughter plays on the floor
with plastic letters,
red, blue & hard yellow,
learning how to spell,
spelling,
how to make spells

———

and I wonder how many women
denied themselves daughters,
closed themselves in rooms,
drew the curtains
so they could mainline words.

———

A child is not a poem,
a poem is not a child.
There is no either/or.
However.

———

I return to the story
of the woman caught in the war
& in labor, her thighs tied

together by the enemy
so she could not give birth.

Ancestress: the burning witch,
her mouth covered by leather
to strangle words.

A word after a word
after a word is power.

————

At the point where language falls away
from the hot bones, at the point
where the rock breaks open and darkness
flows out of it like blood, at
the melting point of granite
when the bones know
they are hollow & the word
splits & doubles & speaks
the truth & the body
itself becomes a mouth.

This is a metaphor.

————

How do you learn to spell?
Blood, sky & the sun,
your own name first,
your first naming, your first name,
your first word.

MARGARET ATWOOD

For Andrew

"Will I die?" you ask. And so I enter on
The dutiful exposition of that which you
Would rather not know, and I rather not tell you.
To soften my "Yes" I offer compensations—
Age and fulfilment ("It's so far away:
You will have children and grandchildren by then")
And indifference ("By then you will not care").
No need: you cannot believe me, convinced
That if you always eat plenty of vegetables
And are careful crossing the street you will live for
     ever.
And so we close the subject, with much unsaid—
This, for instance: Though you and I may die
Tomorrow or next year, and nothing remain
Of our stock, of the unique, preciously hoarded
Inimitable genes we carry in us,
It is possible that for many generations
There will exist, sprung from whatever seeds,
Children straight-limbed, with clear enquiring voices,
Bright-eyed as you. Or so I like to think:
Sharing in this your childish optimism.

FLEUR ADCOCK

For a Five-Year-Old

A snail is climbing up the window-sill
Into your room, after a night of rain.
You call me in to see, and I explain
That it would be unkind to leave it there:
It might crawl to the floor; we must take care
That no one squashes it. You understand,
And carry it outside, with careful hand,
To eat a daffodil.

I see, then, that a kind of faith prevails:
Your gentleness is moulded still by words
From me, who have trapped mice and shot wild birds,
From me, who drowned your kittens, who betrayed
Your closest relatives, and who purveyed
The harshest kind of truth to many another.
But that is how things are: I am your mother,
And we are kind to snails.

FLEUR ADCOCK

Daughter, Daughter

When you peel an egg, leave the skin.
If you jump rope, drop the loop.
A pound of feathers equals a pound
of axes.

Blackbirds don't make good pies.
Fill a fruit pie twice as full.
Tin coughs, glass gargles, sand swallows.

Steal only what you can wear.
Two nickels don't ring like a dime.
Saints come in pints, quarts, gallons.

Step on a crack, break your mother's back;
skip one, break your own.

Seeds are round.
Shells listen.

ALBERTA TURNER

Return

My daughter, ten and brown—another summer
in Arizona with her father—steps
nonchalantly down the ramp as planes
unfurl their ghostly plumes of smoke.
I had forgotten how his legs, dark
and lean as hers, once strode toward me
across a stretch of hammered sand.
And her shoulders, sloped like his, a cotton
blouse scooped so low I can see
her collarbones arched gracefully
as wings, the cruel dip

in the hollow of her throat. And my throat
closes when she smiles, her bangs
blown into a fan around her face, hair
blond as the pampas grass that once waved
wild behind our fence. Whatever held us
together then is broken, dishes
in pieces on the floor, his dead
cigarettes crushed one after another
into the rail of the porch.
Now she opens her arms as he
used to, against a backdrop of blue sky,
so wide I worry she'll float up on these
gusts of clutching wind and disappear,
like a half-remembered dream, into
the perilous future, into the white
heart of the sun.

DORIANNE LAUX

Combing

Bending, I bow my head
And lay my hand upon
Her hair, combing, and think
How women do this for
Each other. My daughter's hair
Curls against the comb,
Wet and fragrant—orange

Parings. Her face, downcast,
Is quiet for one so young.

I take her place. Beneath
My mother's hands I feel
The braids drawn up tight
As a piano wire and singing,
Vinegar-rinsed. Sitting
Before the oven I hear
The orange coils tick
The early hour before school.

She combed her grandmother
Mathilda's hair using
A comb made out of bone.
Mathilda rocked her oak wood
Chair, her face downcast,
Intent on tearing rags
In strips to braid a cotton
Rug from bits of orange
and brown. A simple act,

Preparing hair. Something
Women do for each other,
Plaiting the generations.

GLADYS CARDIFF

From *A Birthday Suite*

Hair

When I was the privileged woman I wiped
The hair from your forehead
With its childish pucker, moist as a washcloth

And when I was queen I brushed and braided it
Pulled it away from your ears at the breakfast table
Your ears as complicated as carnations—

Thus year followed year, like the eyeblink that human
    time
Really is, until you decided
I did it poorly, you could do it better, tighter

Yourself. So you brushed me off
But my nose could reconstruct your ripe scalp-smell,
My palms the raw-silk feel of your springy strands.

When finally you sat in the hairdresser chair,
Child hair chopped off, as loose as brush
Around a clearing where someone is going to build,

I adored your face that rose, abrupt and pure,
A moon rising to survey the planet
By its own lucidity, while my hands

Were like lucky exiles who get away with everything.

Years after the revolution they still recall
The velvet ropes at the opera, that feel

Of utter unmistakable luxury.

ALICIA OSTRIKER

The Dream of My Daughter

Officious, I begin
to brush my daughter's hair,
which is delicate and fair
as a green young fern.

She cries, she cries out
"Mommy, watch it,
I'm sensitive"—
but I'm unmoved, I'm passionate.

Like a large beaked bird
I tear, I tear,
I claw at her hair,
her hair green-golden,

her hair straw-light,
her hair of Rapunzel,
shredding, feathery,
descending around me,

her hair of pollen
which dissolves as I watch
to a thousand cells,
her hair of bees—buzzing, alive—

her hair of poison,
her hair of sun in the hive,
her hair that is melting like wax:
"Mommy, mommy," my daughter weeps,

but ruthless I rip it away—
"Rapunzel, Rapunzel, let down your hair"—
till the curls stream hollow and clear
like an empty river,

and only a few blonde burrs, a dying bush,
are left in the brush.

SANDRA M. GILBERT

Holding On

—So, one by one I pull the lice from your red hair.
One by one I try to split them with my fingernails;

no use, they hold on
as they were taught to. Still, they glisten
like heavenly sparks in the morning light
of the bathroom.

I have to pull extra hard on many of them,
use the turquoise, fine-toothed comb
provided by the pharmacy.
They hold on with all their strength:
each has its individual hair to love,
each pus-colored creature
has a genius plan for not leaving you.

I fling the lice out in the air,
thinking how the world despises them,
the other mothers of Berkeley,
and the teachers who have not appreciated their beauty.

And though I've had to poison them again,
I've always understood them,
I also wanted to get that close,
wanted to cling to you in just that manner,
even go back to heaven with you so we won't
have to address this problem of the separate
you-and-me,
of outer and inner.

I hope we will have our same bodies there
and the lice will have their same bodies,
that each hopeful tear-shaped egg
will be allowed to cling forever, not be pulled
between love's destiny
and a lesser freedom—

BRENDA HILLMAN

Identifying Things

Is diabetes catching, he asks,
middle school braggadocio edged
this time with something else, I can't
quite put my finger on it,
until he tells about the needle,
that kid Jamie, jabbing a needle he had picked up
on the street, punctured far into the flesh
of my son's palm.

Trouble boils a greasy steam into the air.
Whose needle, what kind, whose veins
had it entered? My son, my son, only eleven
years old and the doctor over the phone doesn't help,
his nurse says you bet, plenty to worry about,
and it's not just AIDS we'd want to run tests for,
three strains now of hepatitis, find the needle,
bring in the needle, make sure those boys
find that needle.

                    Under the oaks
a new kind of bird flocks at the feeder,
I have no idea what they are, they swarm
and dart around the perches, on the ground,
they are everywhere, and outside their shrill
wheezing chokes out the drone of trucks on the
        interstate.

So he will teach us death, perhaps.
We will allow him the perfect death.

We will all work on dying
together, we will give him that, and maybe
it won't even happen, maybe the needle
belonged to Jamie, he's a diabetic,
maybe it was just one of his own insulin needles,
probably there is nothing in the world
to worry about, chances are slim, we mustn't
upset our boy, mustn't blow this out
of proportion.

                    I can't identify
the birds. They are too streaked
for goldfinches, they could be
warblers, winter plumage, but their beaks
are a little thicker, I'm just not sure
and none of these walls
line up straight.

When the boys find the needle and take it
to the principal and you stop by school
our kid is most upset because his father
is actually seen by his friends, only nerds have
parents who enter this territory,
he will never live it down, his own father
picking him up in front of his friends,
driving him to the doctor's. Just a little needle,
the kind for pricking a finger for small
blood samples, adults always overreact.
The doctor and the nurses laugh out loud,
at home the walls rise crisp
to the ceiling where the light dances.

And the new birds
are pine siskins, yes, they are,
just a little yellow on the wings and tail,
it helps, it always helps when you know
what things are.

WENDY BARKER

Mothers, Daughters

Through every night we hate,
preparing the next day's
war. She bangs the door.
Her face laps up my own
despair, the sour, brown eyes,
the heavy hair she won't
tie back. She's cruel,
as if my private meanness
found a way to punish us.

We gnaw at each other's
skulls. Give me what's mine.
I'd haul her back, choking
myself in her, herself
in me. There is a book
called *Poisons* on her shelf.
Her room stinks with incense,
animal turds, hamsters

she strokes like silk. They
exercise on the bathroom
floor, and two drop through
the furnace vent. The whole
house smells of the accident,
the hot skins, the small
flesh rotting. Six days
we turn the gas up then
to fry the dead. I'd fry
her head if I could until
she cried love, love me!
All she won't let me do.
Her stringy figure in
the windowed room shares
its thin bones with no one.
Only her shadow on the glass
waits like an older sister.
Now she stalks, leans forward,
concentrates merely on getting
from here to there. Her feet
are bare. I hear her breathe
where I can't get in. If I
break through to her, she will
drive nails into my tongue.

SHIRLEY KAUFMAN

I Have Three Daughters

I have three daughters
Like greengage plums.
They sat all day
Sucking their thumbs.
And more's the pity,
They cried all day,
Why doesn't our mother's brown hair
Turn gray?

I have three daughters
Like three cherries.
They sat at the window
The boys to please.
And they couldn't wait
For their mother to grow old.
Why doesn't our mother's brown hair
Turn to snow?

I have three daughters
In the apple tree
Singing Mama send Daddy
With three young lovers
To take them away from me.

I have three daughters
Like greengage plums,
Sitting all day
And sighing all day

And sucking their thumbs;
Singing, Mama won't you fetch and carry,
And Daddy, won't you let us marry,
Singing, sprinkle snow down on Mama's hair
And lordy, give us our share.

RUTH STONE

A Mother's Hearse

The love of a mother for her child
Is not necessarily a beautiful thing
It can be compounded of pride and show
And exalt the self above every thing.

Oh why is that child so spoilt and horrible?
His mother has never neglected the trouble
Of giving him his will at every turn
And that is why his eyes do burn.

His eyes do burn with a hungry fire
His fingers clutch at the air and do not tire
He is a persecuting force
And as he grows older he grows worse.

And for his sake the friends are put down
And the happy people do not come round,

In pride and hostility against the world
This family upon itself is now curled.

Oh wretched they and wretched the friend
And this will continue without end
And all for a mother's love it was,
I say it were better a mother's hearse.

STEVIE SMITH

To Welcome a Changeling

at 20   my daughter   is still   stealing
flowers   from the neighbor's garden
she arrives   at my door   her moon
face reflecting   mine   yet still filled
with little girl   innocence
a limp rose   in one hand
its blunt   stem   flattened
between thumb   and forefinger
ragged   as her bitten   fingernails

if I could be more   mother   than poet
I would see   only   the flower
but as it is   I shift my load
of metaphors   until   I have sifted
through sad tales   of how many   petals

hold a lover's tears   or how   its fruit
is said to cure   loneliness   or madness
or how she has learned   to pluck
each bud   above   the first thorn

for several years   the neighbors
have watched her   come   and go
watched her   move in   and out   until I
realize all she owns   should be   on wheels
yet each year   I welcome   her return
her stories   of streets   and strangers
root-dark   and sweet   pale   and bitter

she arrives   bearing the hint   of fall
and I watch   her body   casually held inside
curves I've learned   to carefully guard
lean forward to exchange   one
closed-mouth kiss   for one
flower   its stem   bruised and broken
short as our last   conversation
and I chew   the edges   of old poems

where roses   are said to hold
the secrets   of dream times
their petals   crimson   rouge burnished
smooth   as her black skin   and mirroring
her face   and mine   profiling Morocco
the fusci coloris   Zenobia   or Akam
the confusion of flowers   and love
of silence   unbroken

and I try not to remember   how the girls
in my family   arrived at my aunt's
childless   house   one by one
bringing her   our sixteen years   of troubles
or how my house   is now   littered
with bud vases   egg cups   shallow bowls
their surfaces   bruised   with dried bits
of short-stemmed   flowers
their petals   curled   and waiting
each one   like the other

COLLEEN MCELROY

Mother to Son

Well, son, I'll tell you:
Life for me ain't been no crystal stair.
It's had tacks in it,
And splinters,
And boards torn up,
And places with no carpet on the floor—
Bare.
But all the time
I'se been a-climbin' on,
And reachin' landin's,
And turnin' corners,
And sometimes goin' in the dark

Where there ain't been no light.
So boy, don't you turn back.
Don't you set down on the steps
'Cause you finds it's kinder hard.
Don't you fall now—
For I'se still goin', honey,
I'se still climbin',
And life for me ain't been no crystal stair.

LANGSTON HUGHES

Family Reunion

The week in August you come home,
adult, professional, aloof,
we roast and carve the fatted calf
—in our case home-grown pig, the chine
garlicked and crisped, the applesauce
hand-pressed. Hand-pressed the greengage wine.

Nothing is cost-effective here.
The peas, the beets, the lettuces.
hand sown, are raised to stand apart.
The electric fence ticks like the slow heart
of something we fed and bedded for a year,
then killed with kindness's one bullet
and paid Jake Mott to do the butchering.

In winter we lure the birds with suet,
thaw lungs and kidneys for the cat.
Darlings, it's all a circle from the ring
of wire that keeps the raccoons from the corn
to the gouged pine table that we lounge around,
distressed before any of you was born.

Benign and dozy from our gluttonies,
the candles down to stubs, defenses down,
love leaking out unguarded the way
juice dribbles from the fence when grounded
by grass stalks or a forgotten hoe,
how eloquent, how beautiful you seem!

Wearing our gestures, how wise you grow,
ballooning to overfill our space,
the almost-parents of your parents now.
So briefly having you back to measure us
is harder than having let you go.

MAXINE KUMIN

Advice

My hazard wouldn't be yours, not ever;
But every doom, like a hazelnut, comes down
To its own worm. So I am rocking here
Like any granny with her apron over her head
Saying, lordy me. It's my trouble.
There's nothing to be learned this way.
If I heard a girl crying help
I would go to save her;
But you hardly ever hear those words.
Dear children, you must try to say
Something when you are in need.
Don't confuse hunger with greed;
And don't wait until you are dead.

RUTH STONE

IV

THE LOST CHILD: MOTHER GRIEF

There are many ways of losing a child. Poverty and politics, illness and war, stillbirth, abortion, miscarriage—all sever mother from child and all are sources of mother grief. Donne's mourning Niobe represents the sorrow experienced by mothers of dead children from the wife of Usher's well (in the ballad of that name) to the Civil War mother depicted in Walt Whitman's "Come up from the Fields Father." Yet the helpless slave mother who is torn from her child in Frances E. W. Harper's poem, the infertile speaker of Sharon Thesen's "Elegy," and the pained speaker of Anita Barrows's "Miscarriage" suffer comparable anguish.

Death has many faces and the mother often feels in her own body with particular force the truth of Shakespeare's claim that children are "hostages to fortune." *"Grieve not so, dear mother"* urges "the just-grown daughter" in "Come up from the Fields," but like so many bereft women, Whitman's heroine finds herself "in the midnight waking, weeping, longing with one deep longing."

Niobe

By childrens births, and death, I am become
So dry, that I am now mine owne sad tombe.

JOHN DONNE

Elegy, the Fertility Specialist

He gave it to me straight
and I had to thank him
for the information, the percentages
that dwindled in his pencil writing
hand. I watched them drop
from 70, to 40, to 20
as all the variables were added in
and even after 20 he made a question mark. I felt
doors closing in swift silent succession
as I passed each checkpoint on the way
to the cold awful ruler, expert astronomer,
charterer of heavenly colonies,
answerer of questions, and this question
Could we have a child? and this answer, No
I don't think so. Oh
of course he could go in there
and have a look if I really wanted,
steer his ship around the fraying edges

of my terrain, peering with his spyglass,
cross-hatching impediments on his diagram
of the uterine pear & its two branching filaments:
he wouldn't recommend it, he would say,
squeezing his spyglass shut and putting it back
in its maroon velvet box. We make the usual
small gestures of disappointment
as if we'd run out of luck in a ticket line
and I say goodbye
and walk past the receptionist
busy at her files and it is
as if something with wings was crushing itself
to my heart, to comfort
or to be comforted I didn't know which
or even what it was, some angel, and
entered the elevator with the gabbing nurses
going down to lunch and a little girl
in a sun dress, her delicate
golden shoulders stencilled from the lines
of her bathing suit: a perfect white X.

SHARON THESEN

Motherhood

Don't knock on my door, little child,
I cannot let you in;
You know not what a world this is
Of cruelty and sin.
Wait in the still eternity
Until I come to you.
The world is cruel, cruel, child,
I cannot let you through.

Don't knock at my heart, little one,
I cannot bear the pain
Of turning deaf ears to your call,
Time and time again.
You do not know the monster men
Inhabiting the earth.
Be still, be still, my precious child,
I cannot give you birth.

GEORGIA DOUGLAS JOHNSON

The Mother

Abortions will not let you forget.
You remember the children you got that you did not
    get,

The damp small pulps with a little or with no hair,
The singers and workers that never handled the air.
You will never neglect or beat
Them, or silence or buy with a sweet.
You will never wind up the sucking-thumb
Or scuttle off ghosts that come.
You will never leave them, controlling your luscious
    sigh,
Return for a snack of them, with gobbling mother-
    eye.

I have heard in the voices of the wind the voices of my
    dim killed children.
I have contracted. I have eased
My dim dears at the breasts they could never suck.
I have said, Sweets, if I sinned, if I seized
Your luck
And your lives from your unfinished reach,
If I stole your births and your names,
Your straight baby tears and your games,
Your stilted or lovely loves, your tumults, your
    marriages, aches, and your deaths,
If I poisoned the beginnings of your breaths,
Believe that even in my deliberateness I was not
    deliberate.
Though why should I whine,
Whine that the crime was other than mine?—
Since anyhow you are dead.
Or rather, or instead,
You were never made.

But that too, I am afraid,
Is faulty: oh, what shall I say, how is the truth to be
 said?
You were born, you had body, you died.
It is just that you never giggled or planned or cried.

Believe me, I loved you all.
Believe me, I knew you, though faintly, and I loved, I
 loved you
All.

GWENDOLYN BROOKS

The Lost Baby Poem

the time i dropped your almost body down
down to meet the waters under the city
and run one with the sewage to the sea
what did i know about waters rushing back
what did i know about drowning
or being drowned

you would have been born into winter
in the year of the disconnected gas
and no car   we would have made the thin
walk over Genesee hill into the Canada wind
to watch you slip like ice into strangers' hands
you would have fallen naked as snow into winter

if you were here i could tell you these
and some other things

if i am ever less than a mountain
for your definite brothers and sisters
let the rivers pour over my head
let the sea take me for a spiller
of seas   let black men call me stranger
always   for your never named sake

LUCILLE CLIFTON

Miscarriage

That rock has a hole the river ate into it. You can see
how the force of something that keeps on
running overcomes in the end, pitted against
what's solid, & leaves its own shape. That summer
I walked around with the baby dying inside me
I learned to believe that emptiness, too, had a shape.
Blackberries were ripening on Visalia Walk, as far
as the doctor would let me go. Every day there was
    blood
the color of bruised blackberries on my clothes; but
    dark
juice stained my hands, too, even down to the wrist,
    when I'd reach

deep into the stickers for just one more. When
    everyone
went camping or to work, when even the traffic
came to a standstill in midday heat, I picked
& ate, thinking magic like *August, honeysuckle*, thinking
Wait, be safe, don't go yet. Then one afternoon,
heavy with greed & loneliness & the still dissolving
weight inside me, I knew
it could be only hours before the sluice
would open & the last shape
of that baby in this world would be
a purplish widening blot on the bedsheet. I stood
on that flagstone path & stuffed whole handfuls
into my mouth, until the seeds
made a rasping sound crushed by my teeth
like ground rock, until
I was sure that every last ripe one
was gone.

ANITA BARROWS

Maternity

One wept whose only child was dead,
    New-born, ten years ago.
"Weep not; he is in bliss," they said.
    She answered, "Even so,

"Ten years ago was born in pain
A child, not now forlorn.
But oh, ten years ago, in vain,
A mother, a mother was born."

ALICE MEYNELL

Orinda upon Little Hector Philips

Twice forty months of wedlock I did stay,
Then had my vows crown'd with a lovely boy,
And yet in forty days he dropt away;
O swift vicissitude of human joy!

I did but see him, and he disappear'd,
I did but pluck the rosebud and it fell;
A sorrow unforeseen and scarcely fear'd,
For ill can mortals their afflictions spell.

And now (sweet babe!) what can my trembling heart
Suggest to right my doleful fate or thee?
Tears are my Muse, and sorrow all my art,
So piercing groans must be thy elegy.

Thus whilst no eye is witness of my moan,
I grieve thy loss (Ah, boy too dear to live!),
And let the unconcerned world alone,
Who neither will nor can refreshment give.

An off'ring too for thy sad tomb I have,
Too just a tribute to thy early hearse,
Receive these gasping numbers to thy grave,
The last of thy unhappy mother's verse.

KATHERINE PHILIPS

Epitaph on Her Son H.P. at St Syth's Church

What on earth deserves our trust?
Youth and beauty both are dust.
Long we gathering are with pain,
What one moment calls again.
Seven years' childless marriage past,
A son, a son is born at last:
So exactly limbed and fair,
Full of good spirits, mien, and air,
As a long life promised,
Yet, in less than six weeks dead.
Too promising, too great a mind
In so small room to be confined:
Therefore, as fit in Heav'n to dwell,
He quickly broke the prison shell.
So the subtle alchemist
Can't with Hermes' seal resist

The powerful spirit's subtler flight,
But 'twill bid him long good night:
And so the sun, if it arise
Half so glorious as his eyes,
Like this infant, takes a shroud,
Buried in a morning cloud.

KATHERINE PHILIPS

Child Burial

Your coffin looked unreal,
fancy as a wedding cake.

I chose your grave clothes with care,
your favourite stripey shirt,

your blue cotton trousers.
They smelt of woodsmoke, of October,

your own smell there too.
I chose a gansy of handspun wool,

warm and fleecy for you. It is
so cold down in the dark.

No light can reach you and teach you
the paths of wild birds,

the names of the flowers,
the fishes, the creatures.

Ignorant you must remain
of the sun and its work,

my lamb, my calf, my eaglet,
my cub, my kid, my nestling,

my suckling, my colt. I would spin
time back, take you again

within my womb, your amniotic lair,
and further spin you back

through nine waxing months
to the split seeding moment

you chose to be made flesh,
word within me.

I'd cancel the love feast
the hot night of your making.

I would travel alone
to a quiet mossy place,

you would spill from me into the earth
drop by bright red drop.

PAULA MEEHAN

In Memory of My Dear Grandchild Anne Bradstreet
Who Deceased June 20, 1669,
Being Three Years and Seven Months Old

With troubled heart and trembling hand I write,
The heavens have changed to sorrow my delight.
How oft with disappointment have I met,
When I on fading things my hopes have set?
Experience might 'fore this have made me wise,
To value things according to their price.
Was ever stable joy yet found below?
Or perfect bliss without mixture of woe?
I knew she was but as a withering flower,
That's here today, perhaps gone in an hour;
Like as a bubble, or the brittle glass,
Or like a shadow turning as it was.
More fool then I to look on that was lent
As if mine own, when thus impermanent.
Farewell dear child, thou ne'er shall come to me,
But yet a while, and I shall go to thee;
Mean time my throbbing heart's cheered up with this:
Thou with thy Saviour art in endless bliss.

ANNE BRADSTREET

On the Death of an Infant of Five Years Old

Dear pretty babe farewell, a blest adieu;
Wou'd I were half as blest, as guiltless too.
For thee, dear angel, tho' we drop a tear,
Thy certain happiness dispels our fear;
So when the innocents by Herod died,
More saints rejoic'd than earthly mothers cry'd.

ELIZABETH BOYD

The Slave Mother

Heard you that shriek? It rose
    So wildly on the air,
It seemed as if a burden'd heart
    Was breaking in despair.

Saw you those hands so sadly clasped—
    The bowed and feeble head—
The shuddering of that fragile form—
    That look of grief and dread?

Saw you the sad, imploring eye?
    Its every glance was pain,
As if a storm of agony
    Were sweeping through the brain.

She is a mother, pale with fear,
    Her boy clings to her side,
And in her kirtle vainly tries
    His trembling form to hide.

He is not hers, although she bore
    For him a mother's pains;
He is not hers, although her blood
    Is coursing through his veins!

He is not hers, for cruel hands
    May rudely tear apart
The only wreath of household love
    That binds her breaking heart.

His love has been a joyous light
    That o'er her pathway smiled,
A fountain gushing ever new,
    Amid life's desert wild.

His lightest word has been a tone
    Of music round her heart,
Their lives a streamlet blent in one—
    Oh, Father! must they part?

They tear him from her circling arms,
    Her last and fond embrace.
Oh! never more may her sad eyes
    Gaze on his mournful face.

No marvel, then, these bitter shrieks
    Disturb the listening air:
She is a mother, and her heart
    Is breaking in despair.

Frances E. W. Harper

Declared Not Fit

In this month of grief I am crying for my lover.
Suddenly my children appear under my closed eyelids
inside my grief, as if in a pitch-dark room,
vision: apparitions heavy with distance, absence.

I think: This is how you see your past just
before you die.

           My eyes were the rearview mirror
years ago.   The boys were small and round, waving
good-bye.   Their eyes were the young eyes of children
looking at their mother, that she will explain.

What were the reasons?   Power of a man over
a woman, his children: his hand on power he lacked,
that my womb had made children as the eye makes a
    look.

129

What were the reasons?   Terror of a man left alone,
the terror at a gesture: my hand sliding from her
soft pulse neck, to jawbone, chin, mouth met,
mouth of sharp salt.   We walked the barrier island,
us, the two boys, the skittering orange crabs,
public deserted beach.   In front of the children.

The danger: eyes taught not to cringe away,
the power of their eyes drawn to our joined hands.
Filthy, unfit, not to touch:
                                                 those from my womb,
red birthslime, come by my cry of agony and pleasure.

Hands smeared often enough with their shit, vomit,
blackness of dirt and new blood, but water from my
        hands,
and in them, weight of their new bodies come back to
        rest.

When behind the closed eyelid of a door, in the heavy
        bed,
sweaty, salty, frantic and calling out sublimely
another woman's name, hands unclenched, I brought
        down
a cry of joy, then my mouth, mind, hands became
not fit to touch.

                            The work is the same.

What are the reasons?   I told them these.
They were young, they did not understand.

Nor do I.   Words heard in the ear, hollow room.
The eye waits, sad, unsatisfied,
to embrace the particular loved shape.
Eyes, empty   hands, empty   waiting.

MINNIE BRUCE PRATT

Mother and Poet

Turin, after News from Gaeta, 1861

I

Dead! One of them shot by the sea in the east,
    And one of them shot in the west by the sea.
Dead! both my boys! When you sit at the feast
    And are wanting a great song for Italy free,
    Let none look at *me!*

II

Yet I was a poetess only last year,
    And good at my art, for a woman, men said;
But *this* woman, *this,* who is agonized here,
    —The east sea and west sea rhyme on in her head
    For ever instead.

III

What art can a woman be good at? Oh, vain!
    What art *is* she good at, but hurting her breast

With the milk-teeth of babes, and a smile at the pain?
    Ah boys, how you hurt! you were strong as you
      pressed,
    And I proud, by that test.

IV

What art's for a woman? To hold on her knees
    Both darlings! to feel all their arms round her throat,
Cling, strangle a little! to sew by degrees
    And 'broider the long-clothes and neat little coat;
    To dream and to doat.

V

To teach them . . . It stings there! *I* made them indeed
    Speak plain the word *country*. *I* taught them, no
      doubt,
That a country's a thing men should die for at need.
    I prated of liberty, rights, and about
    The tyrant cast out.

VI

And when their eyes flashed . . . O my beautiful eyes! . . .
    I exulted: nay, let them go forth at the wheels
Of the guns, and denied not. But then the surprise
    When one sits quite alone! Then one weeps, then
      one kneels!
    God, how the house feels!

VII

At first, happy news came, in gay letters moiled
    With my kisses,—of camp-life and glory, and how
They both loved me; and, soon coming home to be
      spoiled
    In return would fan off every fly from my brow
    With their green laurel-bough.

VIII

Then was triumph at Turin: "Ancona was free!"
    And some one came out of the cheers in the street,
With a face pale as stone, to say something to me.
    My Guido was dead! I fell down at his feet,
    While they cheered in the street.

IX

I bore it; friends soothed me; my grief looked sublime
    As the ransom of Italy. One boy remained
To be leant on and walked with, recalling the time
    When the first grew immortal, while both of us
      strained
    To the height he had gained.

X

And letters still came, shorter, sadder, more strong,
    Writ now but in one hand, "I was not to faint,—
One loved me for two—would be with me ere long:

133

And *Viva l'Italia!*—*he* died for, our saint,
Who forbids our complaint."

XI

My Nanni would add, "he was safe, and aware
    Of a presence that turned off the balls,—was imprest
It was Guido himself, who knew what I could bear,
    And how 't was impossible, quite dispossessed
    To live on for the rest."

XII

On which, without pause, up the telegraph line
    Swept smoothly the next news from Gaeta:—*Shot.*
Tell his mother. Ah, ah, "his," "their" mother,—not
    "mine,"
    No voice says *"My* mother" again to me. What!
    You think Guido forgot?

XIII

Are souls straight so happy that, dizzy with Heaven,
    They drop earth's affections, conceive not of woe?
I think not. Themselves were too lately forgiven
    Through THAT Love and Sorrow which reconciled so
    The Above and Below.

XIV

O Christ of the five wounds, who look'dst through the
    dark

To the face of thy mother! consider, I pray,
How we common mothers stand desolate, mark,
  Whose sons, not being Christs, die with eyes turned
    away,
  And no last word to say!

XV

Both boys dead? but that's out of nature. We all
  Have been patriots, yet each house must always keep
    one.
'Twere imbecile, hewing out roads to a wall;
  And, when Italy's made, for what end is it done
  If we have not a son?

XVI

Ah, ah, ah! when Gaeta's taken, what then?
  When the fair wicked queen sits no more at her
    sport
Of the fire-balls of death crashing souls out of men?
  When the guns of Cavalli with final retort
  Have cut the game short?

XVII

When Venice and Rome keep their new jubilee,
  When your flag takes all heaven for its white, green,
    and red,
When *you* have your country from mountain to sea,

When King Victor has Italy's crown on his head,
(And *I* have my dead)—

XVIII

What then? Do not mock me. Ah, ring your bells low,
    And burn your lights faintly! *My* country is *there,*
Above the star pricked by the last peak of snow:
    My Italy's THERE, with my brave civic pair,
      To disfranchise despair!

XIX

Forgive me. Some women bear children in strength,
    And bite back the cry of their pain in self-scorn;
But the birth-pangs of nations will wring us at length
    Into wail such as this—and we sit on forlorn
      When the man-child is born.

XX

Dead! One of them shot by the sea in the east,
    And one of them shot in the west by the sea.
Both! both my boys! If in keeping the feast
    You want a great song for your Italy free,
      Let none look at *me!*

ELIZABETH BARRETT BROWNING

Come up from the Fields Father

Come up from the fields father, here's a letter from our
    Pete,
And come to the front door mother, here's a letter from
    thy dear son.

Lo, 'tis autumn,
Lo, where the trees, deeper green, yellower and redder,
Cool and sweeten Ohio's villages with leaves fluttering
    in the moderate wind,
Where apples ripe in the orchards hang and grapes on
    the trellis'd vines
(Smell you the smell of the grapes on the vines?
Smell you the buckwheat where the bees were lately
    buzzing?)

Above all, lo, the sky so calm, so transparent after the
    rain, and with wondrous clouds,
Below too, all calm, all vital and beautiful, and the farm
    prospers well.

Down in the fields all prospers well,
But now from the fields come father, come at the
    daughter's call,
And come to the entry mother, to the front door come
    right away.

Fast as she can she hurries, something ominous, her
    steps trembling,

She does not tarry to smooth her hair nor adjust her
    cap.

Open the envelope quickly,
O this is not our son's writing, yet his name is sign'd,
O a strange hand writes for our dear son, O stricken
    mother's soul!
All swims before her eyes, flashes with black, she
    catches the main words only,
Sentences broken, *gunshot wound in the breast, cavalry
    skirmish, taken to hospital,*
At present low, but will soon be better.

Ah now the single figure to me,
Amid all teeming and wealthy Ohio with all its cities
    and farms,
Sickly white in the face and dull in the head, very faint,
By the jamb of a door leans.

Grieve not so, dear mother, (the just-grown daughter speaks
    through her sobs,
The little sisters huddle around speechless and
    dismay'd,)
See, dearest mother, the letter says Pete will soon be better.

Alas poor boy, he will never be better, (nor may-be
    needs to be better, that brave and simple soul,)
While they stand at home at the door he is dead
    already,
The only son is dead.

But the mother needs to be better,
She with thin form presently drest in black,
By day her meals untouch'd, then at night fitfully
   sleeping, often waking,
In the midnight waking, weeping, longing with one
   deep longing,
O that she might withdraw unnoticed, silent from life
   escape and withdraw,
To follow, to seek, to be with her dear dead son.

WALT WHITMAN

Upon the gallows hung a wretch

Upon the gallows hung a wretch,
Too sullied for the hell
To which the law entitled him.
As nature's curtain fell
The one who bore him tottered in,—
For this was woman's son.
" 'Twas all I had," she stricken gasped—
Oh, what a livid boon!

EMILY DICKINSON

The Wife of Usher's Well

There lived a wife at Usher's Well,
    And a wealthy wife was she;
She had three stout and stalwart sons,
    And sent them o'er the sea.

They hadna' been a week from her,
    A week but barely ane,
When word came to the carlin wife
    That her three sons were gane.

They hadna' been a week from her,
    A week but barely three,

When word came to the carlin wife
    That her sons she'd never see.

"I wish the wind may never cease
    Nor fashes in the flood,
Till my three sons come hame to me,
    In earthly flesh and blood."

It fell about the Martinmas,
    When nights are long and mirk,
The carlin wife's three sons came hame,
    And their hats were o' the birk.

It neither grew in sike nor ditch,
    Nor yet in ony sheugh,
But at the gates o' Paradise
    That birk grew fair eneugh.

"Blow up the fire, my maidens,
    Bring water from the well:
For a' my house shall feast this night,
    Since my three sons are well."

And she has made to them a bed,
    She's made it large and wide,
And she's ta'en her mantle her about,
    Sat down at the bedside.

Up then crew the red, red cock,
    And up and crew the gray.

The eldest to the youngest said,
  " 'Tis time we were away."

The cock he hadna' crawed but once,
    And clapped his wings at a',
When the youngest to the eldest said,
    "Brother, we must awa'.

"The cock doth craw, the day doth daw,
    The channerin' worm doth chide:
Gin we be missed out o' our place,
    A sair pain we maun bide.

"Fare ye weel, my mother dear,
    Fareweel to barn and byre.
And fare ye weel, the bonny lass
    That kindles my mother's fire."

ANONYMOUS

My Boy Jack

"Have you news of my boy Jack?"
        Not this tide.
"When d'you think that he'll come back?"
        Not with this wind blowing, and this tide.

142

"Has any one else had word of him?"
  Not this tide.
For what is sunk will hardly swim,
  Not with this wind blowing, and this tide.

"Oh, dear, what comfort can I find?"
  None this tide,
  Nor any tide,
Except he did not shame his kind—
  Not even with that wind blowing, and that tide.

Then hold your head up all the more,
  This tide,
  And every tide;
Because he was the son you bore,
  And gave to that wind blowing and that tide!

RUDYARD KIPLING

V

*I*N THE FLOOD
OF REMEMBRANCE:
STORIES ABOUT OUR
MOTHERS

*M*others influence us at every point in our lives; they appear positively as teachers, enhancers, helpers, guides; negatively as rivals, cautions, and fears. The stories about them endure to become sources of strength, examples of method, reminders of love, warnings against failure. These stories are repeated because they hold lessons that have become part of us.

Mothers are celebrated in poems of memory and they are mourned in them as well: ". . . til the heart of me weeps to belong," D. H. Lawrence says in "Piano." Sometimes the fruit of recollection is anger, as in Judith Hemschemeyer's "The Survivors"; sometimes it is understanding of the past, as in C. K. Williams's "My Mother's Lips" or Louise Gluck's "Widows," where the poet explains that "the one who has nothing wins."

Even in disarray and at odds with her child the mother remembered is a powerful figure. "Her hacksaw rage/whistled clean to the bone" recalls Karen Fizer in "Implicature." She intrudes on our dreams and achievements, on our efforts to adjust our lives; she demands to have her story told, as it is told here, from many standpoints and in many voices, by her children.

Piano

Softly, in the dusk, a woman is singing to me;
Taking me back down the vista of years, till I see
A child sitting under the piano, in the boom of the
    tingling strings
And pressing the small, poised feet of a mother who
    smiles as she sings.

In spite of myself, the insidious mastery of song
Betrays me back, till the heart of me weeps to belong
To the old Sunday evenings at home, with winter
    outside
And hymns in the cosy parlour, the tinkling piano our
    guide.

So now it is vain for the singer to burst into clamour
With the great black piano appassionato. The glamour
Of childish days is upon me, my manhood is cast
Down in the flood of remembrance, I weep like a child
    for the past.

D. H. LAWRENCE

Nurse

My mother went to work each day
in a starched white dress, shoes
clamped to her feet like pale
mushrooms, two blue hearts pressed
into the sponge rubber soles.
When she came back home, her nylons
streaked with runs, a spatter
of blood across her bodice,
she sat at one end of the dinner table
and let us kids serve the spaghetti, sprinkle
the parmesan, cut the buttered loaf.
We poured black wine into the bell
of her glass as she unfastened
her burgundy hair, shook her head, and began.
And over the years we mastered it, how to listen
to stories of blocked intestines
while we twirled the pasta, of saws
teething cranium, drills boring holes in bone
as we crunched the crust of our sourdough,
carved the stems off our cauliflower.
We learned the importance of balance,
how an operation depends on
cooperation and a blend of skills,
the art of passing the salt
before it is asked for.
She taught us well, so that when Mary Ellen
ran the iron over her arm, no one wasted
a moment: My brother headed straight for the ice.

Our little sister uncapped the salve.
And I dialed the number under Ambulance,
my stomach turning to the smell
of singed skin, already planning the evening
meal, the raw fish thawing in its wrapper,
a perfect wedge of flesh.

DORIANNE LAUX

I Remember Haifa Being Lovely But

there were snakes in the
tent, my mother was
strong but she never
slept, was afraid of
dreaming. In Auschwitz
there was a numbness,
lull of just staying
alive. Her two babies
gassed before her, Dr.
Mengele, you know who
he is? She kept her
young sister alive
only to have her die
in her arms the night
of liberation. My mother
is big boned, but she

weighed under 80 lbs.
It was hot, I thought
the snakes lovely. No
drugs in Israel, no
food. I got pneumonia,
my mother knocked the
doctor to the floor
when they refused,
said I lost two in
the camp and if this
one dies I'll kill
myself in front of
you. I thought that
once you became a
mother, blue numbers
appeared mysteriously,
tattooed on your arm

LYN LIFSHIN

No Quarrels Today

Mother carried a washbasin
into the bathroom and placed it in the bathtub.
She wrapped her apron around her waist
like she meant business, tied a bandanna on her head,
and crossed herself like a bullfighter

before a shrine of the Virgin. We knew we had to be
    careful
because this was New Year's Eve,
the day she made tamales
and, as she warned us every year,
if there was a harsh word in the house,
the tamales would not be good.

When Teresa locked herself in the car
and her husband punched the windshield,
the tamales were no good.
The time I made fun of my niece
because she was cross-eyed, and I scared my sister
by standing like a zombie in her closet,
the tamales were no good.
When Titi Rosa took a swing at Guillermo
with her cane, when everyone called Johnny a drunk
because he fell asleep beneath the Christmas tree
with his head in the *nacimiento*, and Richie
was telling each guest that my mother missed
while trying to spit in the bathtub and it landed in the
    masa,
the tamales were no good.

Every year we laughed, but not too loud,
Nobody crossed my mother. My older brother,
a grown man with a wife and children,
had to come to her and beg forgiveness on his knees.
Not a figure of speech, but on his knees.
If you asked her to throw the *cartas*

you had better be prepared for the truth.
Once she looked up from the ace of spades
and told Vicente, "Go home, get your house in order,"
and he was dead in a week.
When she said to Rachel, who was poor as a mouse,
"You will take a trip across the ocean and fall in love
    on the ship,"
Rachel went straight to the beauty parlor.

That is why we tiptoed around and said please and
    excuse me,
why we did not make jokes about the saints
or sit in the dark staring in the mirror hoping to see
    the devil.
Why at one in the morning the party got quiet
when we carried out two steaming tins from the
    kitchen,
each with one hundred tamales, some with chicken,
    chile,
and two olives, some sweet with honey and corn.
It was New Year's and my sister Inez's birthday
and even strangers who came to our party by mistake
came back every year. And everyone sitting around our
    house,
from the *sala* to the *cucurucho*, eating Cuka's famous
    tamales,
knew we had behaved ourselves, at least for one day,
because the tamales were good.

RICHARD GARCIA

During Fever

All night the crib creaks;
home from the healthy country to the sick city,
my daughter in fever
flounders in her chicken-colored sleeping bag.
"Sorry," she mumbles like her dim-bulb father, "sorry."

Mother, Mother!
as a gemlike undergraduate,
part criminal and yet a Phi Bete,
I used to barge home late.
Always by the banister
my milk-tooth mug of milk
was waiting for me on a plate
of Triskets.
Often with unadulterated joy,
Mother, we bent by the fire
rehashing Father's character—
when he thought we were asleep,
he'd tiptoed down the stairs
and chain the door.

Mother, your master-bedroom
looked away from the ocean.
You had a window-seat,
an electric blanket,
a silver hot-water bottle
monogrammed like a hip-flask,
Italian china fruity

with bunches and berries
and proper *putti.*
Gold, yellow and green,
the nuptial bed
was as big as a bathroom.
Born ten years and yet an aeon
too early for the twenties,
Mother, you smile
as if you saw your Father
inches away yet hidden, as when he groused behind a
    screen
over a National Geographic Magazine,
whenever young men came to court you
back in those settled years of World War One.
Terrible that old life of decency
without unseemly intimacy
or quarrels, when the unemancipated woman
still had her Freudian papá and maids!

ROBERT LOWELL

From a Heart of Rice Straw

Ma, my heart must be made of rice straw,
the kind you fed a fire in Papa's home village
so Grandma could have hot tea upon waking,
so Grandma could wash her sleepy eyes. My heart
knocks as silently as that LeCoultre clock
that Papa bought with his birthday money.
It swells like a baby in your stomach.

Your tears have flooded the house, this life.
For Canton? No, you left home forty years ago
for the fortune Papa sought in Gum San.
In Gold Mountain you worked side by side
in the lottery with regular pay offs
to the Oakland cops. To feed your six daughters
until one day Papa's cousin shot him.

I expected you to fly into the clouds, wail
at Papa's side, but you chased cousin instead.
Like the cops and robbers on the afternoon radio.
It didn't matter that Papa lay bleeding.
It didn't matter that cousin accused Papa
of cheating him. You ran, kicking
your silk slippers on the street, chasing
cousin until you caught him, gun still in hand.
My sister and I followed you, crying.

If cousin had shot you, you would have died.
The cops showed up and you told them how cousin

gunned Papa down, trusted kin who smoked
Havana cigars after filling his belly with rice
and chicken in our big yellow house.

Papa lay in his hospital bed, his kidney removed.
Three bullets out. They couldn't find the last
bullet. A search was made, hands dove into Papa's
shirt pocket. A gold watch saved Papa's life.

Ma, you've told this story one hundred times.
The cops said you were brave. The neighbors said
you were brave. The relatives shook their heads,
the bravery of a Gold Mountain woman unknown
in the old home village.

The papers spread the shooting all over town.
One said Papa dueled with his brother like
a bar room brawl. One said it was the beginning
of a tong war, but that Occidental law
would prevail. To them, to the outside,
what was another tong war, another dead Chinaman?

But Papa fooled them. He did not die
by his cousin's hand. The lottery closed down.
We got food on credit. You wept.
I was five years old.

My heart, once bent and cracked, once
ashamed of your China ways.

Ma, hear me now, tell me your story
again and again.

NELLIE WONG

The Survivors

Night after night
She dreamed we were drowned
Or covered with spiders
Or butchered or tortured

She took us all to bed with her

And woke up whimpering
And came to find our bodies
In the dark, brushing our foreheads
Sorting out our tangled limbs

Amazed to find us whole

By day her love for us
Was a prairie fire
That roared across our whole horizon
Burning us out of our burrows

"I touched the windowpane"
"I touched myself"
"I let the boys touch me"

Like small, crazed animals
We leaped before her
Knowing there was no escape

She had to consume us utterly
Over and over again
And now at last
We are her angels
Burned so crisp
We crumble when we try to touch

JUDITH HEMSCHEMEYER

My Mother's Lips

Until I asked her to please stop doing it and was
    astonished to find that she not only could
but from the moment I asked her in fact would stop
    doing it, my mother, all through my childhood,
when I was saying something to her, something
    important, would move her lips as I was speaking
so that she seemed to be saying under her breath the
    very words I was saying as I was saying them.

Or, even more disconcertingly—wildly so now that my
    puberty had erupted—*before* I said them.
When I was smaller, I must just have assumed that she
    was omniscient. Why not?
She knew everything else—when I was tired, or lying;
    she'd know I was ill before I did.
I may even have thought—how could it not have come
    into my mind?—that she *caused* what I said.

All she was really doing of course was mouthing my
    words a split second after I said them myself,
but it wasn't until my own children were learning to
    talk that I really understood how,
and understood, too, the edge of anxiety in it, the
    wanting to bring you along out of the silence,
the compulsion to lift you again from those blank
    caverns of namelessness we encase.

That was long afterward, though: where I was now was
    just wanting to get her to stop,
and, considering how I brooded and raged in those
    days, how quickly my teeth went on edge,
the restraint I approached her with seems remarkable,
    although her so unprotestingly,
readily taming a habit by then three children and a
    dozen years old was as much so.

It's endearing to watch us again in that long-ago dusk,
    facing each other, my mother and me.

I've just grown to her height, or just past it: there are
    our lips moving together,
now the unison suddenly breaks, I have to go on by
    myself, no maestro, no score to follow.
I wonder what finally made me take umbrage enough,
    or heart enough, to confront her?

It's not important. My cocoon at that age was already
    unwinding: the threads ravel and snarl.
When I find one again, it's that two o'clock in the
    morning, a grim hotel on a square,
the impenetrable maze of an endless city, when, really
    alone for the first time in my life,
I found myself leaning from the window, incanting in a
    tearing whisper what I thought were poems.

I'd love to know what I raved that night to the night,
    what those innocent dithyrambs were,
or to feel what so ecstatically drew me out of myself
    and beyond . . . Nothing is there, though,
only the solemn piazza beneath me, the riot of dim,
    tiled roofs and impassable alleys,
my desolate bed behind me, and my voice, hoarse, and
    the sweet, alien air against me like a kiss.

                                        C. K. WILLIAMS

The Night Before Good-bye

Mama is mending
my underwear
while my brothers sleep.
Her husband taken away by the FBI
one son lured away by the Army
now another son and daughter
lusting for the free world outside.
She must let go.
The war goes on.
She will take one still small son
and join Papa in internment
to make a family.
Still sewing
squinting in the dim light
in room C barrack 4 block 4
she whispers
Remember
keep your underwear
in good repair
in case of accident
don't bring shame
on us.

MITSUYE YAMADA

Cactus

For my mother,
Rose Perczykow Klepfisz

The pot itself was half the story.
A yellow ceramic dime store knickknack
of a featureless Mexican
with a large sombrero   pushing a wagon
filled with dirt.

The cactus was the other half.
Self-effacing   it didn't demand much
which was just as well
since she had no spare time
for delicate cultivation.
Used to just the bare essentials
it stood on our kitchen windowsill
two floors above the inhospitable soil
and neither flourished   grew
nor died.

I'd catch her eyeing it
as she stood   breathless
broiling our dinner's minute steaks
her profile centered in the windowframe.
She understood   the meaning   of both pot
and plant   still would insist there was
something extra   the colors yellow
green   or as she once explained

in her stiff   night school English:
"It is always   of importance to see
the things aesthetical."

IRENA KLEPFISZ

Frying Trout While Drunk

Mother is drinking to forget a man
Who could fill the woods with invitations:
Come with me he whispered and she went
In his Nash Rambler, its dash
Where her knees turned green
In the radium dials of the '50s.
When I drink it is always 1953,
Bacon wilting in the pan on Cook Street
And mother, wrist deep in red water,
Laying a trail from the sink
To a glass of gin and back.
She is a beautiful, unlucky woman
In love with a man of lechery so solid
You could build a table on it
And when you did the blues would come to visit.
I remember all of us awkwardly at dinner,
The dark slung across the porch,
And then mother's dress falling to the floor,
Buttons ticking like seeds spit on a plate.
When I drink I am too much like her—

The knife in one hand and in the other
The trout with a belly white as my wrist.
I have loved you all my life
She told him and it was true
In the same way that all her life
She drank, dedicated to the act itself,
She stood at this stove
And with the care of the very drunk
Handed him the plate.

LYNN EMANUEL

Implicature

When my mother cursed me
she was wearing white gloves
as all Southern ladies did
on large occasions.

We were in the red clay
cemetery, us two and Tennessee
Williams, searching for the lost
baby's grave in the hot grass.

Mother stalked the graves,
her skinny cracker body
in that hard green dress, air
gone the high white of noon,

me stumbling along behind her.
Mama, let's just go home.
Let's us just go home.
She turned her toppled face

to me: You don't know how
to love, you never will
know how. Her hacksaw rage
whistled clean to the bone.

KAREN FIZER

The Intruder

My mother—preferring the strange to the tame:
Dove-note, bone marrow, deer dung,
Frog's belly distended with finny young,
Leaf-mould wilderness, hare-bell, toadstool,
Odd, small snakes roving through the leaves,
Metallic beetles rambling over stones: all
Wild and natural!—flashed out her instinctive love, and
    quick, she
Picked up the fluttering, bleeding bat the cat laid at her
    feet,
And held the little horror to the mirror, where
He gazed on himself, and shrieked like an old screen
    door far off.

Depended from her pinched thumb, each wing
Came clattering down like a small black shutter.
Still tranquil, she began, "It's rather sweet. . . ."
The soft mouse body, the hard feral glint
In the caught eyes. Then we saw,
And recoiled: lice, pallid, yellow,
Nested within the wing-pits, cosily sucked and
     snoozed.
The thing dropped from her hands, and with its thud,
Swiftly, the cat, with a clean careful mouth
Closed on the soiled webs, growling, took them out to
     the back stoop.

But still, dark blood, a sticky puddle on the floor
Remained, of all my mother's tender, wounding passion
For a whole wild, lost, betrayed and secret life
Among its dens and burrows, its clean stones,
Whose denizens can turn upon the world
With spitting tongue, an odor, talon, claw,
To sting or soil benevolence, alien
As our clumsy traps, our random scatter of shot.
She swept to the kitchen. Turning on the tap,
She washed and washed the pity from her hands.

                                        CAROLYN KIZER

Widows

My mother's playing cards with my aunt,
Spite and Malice, the family pastime, the game
my grandmother taught all her daughters.

Midsummer: too hot to go out.
Today, my aunt's ahead; she's getting the good cards.
My mother's dragging, having trouble with her
    concentration.
She can't get used to her own bed this summer.
She had no trouble last summer,
getting used to the floor. She learned to sleep there
to be near my father.
He was dying; he got a special bed.

My aunt doesn't give an inch, doesn't make
allowance for my mother's weariness.
It's how they were raised: you show respect by
    fighting.
To let up insults the opponent.

Each player has one pile to the left, five cards in the
    hand.
It's good to stay inside on days like this,
to stay where it's cool.
And this is better than other games, better than
    solitaire.

My grandmother thought ahead; she prepared her
    daughters.
They have cards; they have each other.
They don't need any more companionship.

All afternoon the game goes on but the sun doesn't
    move.
It just keeps beating down, turning the grass yellow.
That's how it must seem to my mother.
And then, suddenly, something is over.

My aunt's been at it longer; maybe that's why she's
    playing better.
Her cards evaporate: that's what you want, that's the
    object: in the end,
the one who has nothing wins.

LOUISE GLÜCK

*My Mother with Purse the Summer They Murdered the
Spanish Poet*

Had she looked out the window she would have seen a
    quiet street,
each house with a single maple or elm browning in the
    sun

at the end of summer, the black Fords and Plymouths
    gleaming
in their fresh wax, the neighbor children returning
    home
dark suited or white frocked from their Christian
    studies.

Had she looked out she would have seen the world she
    crossed
the world to find. Instead she unclasps the leather purse
to make sure she has everything: mirror, lipstick,
    billfold,
her cards of identity, her checkbook with the week's
    balance
correctly entered, two monogramed, embroidered
    handkerchiefs

to blot and hold the tears, for—dark veiled—she's on
    her way
to meet her husband, gone three years now into the sour
    earth
of Michigan. Can the long white root a man in time
    becomes
talk back to one who chose to stay on the far shore
of his departure? Before the day ends, she'll find out.

She will hunch over tea leaves, she will open her palms,
first the hardened hand of the wage earner, then the soft
    one
that opens to the heart. To see, she will close her eyes;

to hear, she will stop her ears, and the words will be
wrong or no words at all, teeth striking teeth, the
        tongue

doubled back upon itself, the blackened lips vanished
into the hole of the throat. But for now she looks up.
It is summer, 1936. The first hints of autumn
mist on a row of curtained windows that look in on us
as my mother, perfumed, leans down to brush my
        mouth with hers,

once, to say my name, precisely, in English. Later
two women will pretend they have reached two other
        worlds,
the one behind and the one ahead. As they keen
in the darkness perhaps only one will pretend, perhaps
neither, for who shall question that we most clearly see

where no eye is? Wide-eyed he sees nothing. White shirt
worn open, dark trousers with no belt, the olive skin
        appalled.
When the same wind he loved and sang to touches his
        cheek
he tries to rub it away. There are others, too, walking
        over
the fat, gray stones to where a line of men smokes and
        waits.

The trees have stilled. Had she looked out the window
my mother would have seen each house with its elm or
        maple

burning, the children drowning in the end of summer,
    the mist
blurring the eyes of our front windows, the shale hills
above Granada where all time stopped. Her purse snaps
    shut.

PHILIP LEVINE

VI

A WOMAN
IS HER MOTHER:
MY MOTHER/MY
SELF

*O*ur common blood": Cynthia Macdonald's
phrase expresses her ambivalent identification with her
mother, ambivalent because the acknowledgment of
resemblance breeds a revulsion for the mother that
teeters into self-loathing. By contrast, Carolyn Kizer
views the similarities between her mother, herself, and
her daughter as a blessing. Many of the poets in this sec-
tion ask daughterly questions: can I define myself only
by differentiating myself from the mother? Does such a
sense of difference contribute to anger at or even hatred
of the mother? Or is my anger, my hatred really a sign
that I am quickly becoming (just like) her? Many writers

meditate on the complicated emotional fallout of Anne Sexton's insight that "a woman *is* her mother."

Of course in most societies, children of both sexes gain their identities by separating from that first other, the mother. Such a need to struggle against early dependency may easily generate the sort of anxiety Sharon Olds and Diane Wakoski voice here, namely a dread of being constructed as the mother's "creature" with a face that reflects the mother's bitterness. But if, as Nancy Chodorow has suggested, mothers tend to relate more empathetically to their daughters, then the boundaries between mother and daughter can blur; daughterly complaints may multiply more frequently than those of sons because young women dread an intimacy or even a sense of interidentification that feels symbiotic. Still, no matter how ferociously the poets in this section seem to have rejected the mother—determining like Marilyn Hacker, "Whatever she was, I was not"—there remains the suspicion that matrophobia (fear of the mother) must inevitably shadow matrophilia (love of the mother).

Housewife

Some women marry houses.
It's another kind of skin; it has a heart,
a mouth, a liver and bowel movements.
The walls are permanent and pink.
See how she sits on her knees all day,
faithfully washing herself down.
Men enter by force, drawn back like Jonah
into their fleshy mothers.
A woman *is* her mother.
That's the main thing.

ANNE SEXTON

Inheritance

I see my mother's last breath
Which has not been drawn
In pen and ink, its jagged graph scrawled on my face,
Crossing out my features
With her lines.
Her lines come out of my mouth so that I discuss
The appearance of the neighbor's children,
The dirty streets of New York
And love, in the same tone of smooth disapproval.
Disapproval sours

My skin into hers,
Implants her congealed brown eyes, her long nose to
Look down, her lips
Like the edges of oysters.

Once a day I sandpaper my features. The swelling
Has obliterated both of us. The basin
On my lap catches our common blood.

CYNTHIA MACDONALD

For My Mother

It was better when we were
together in one body.
Thirty years. Screened
through the green glass
of your eye, moonlight
filtered into my bones
as we lay
in the big bed, in the dark,
waiting for my father.
Thirty years. He closed
your eyelids with
two kisses. And then spring
came and withdrew from me
the absolute

knowledge of the unborn,
leaving the brick stoop
where you stand, shading
your eyes, but it is
night, the moon
is stationed in the beech tree,
round and white among
the small tin markers of the stars:
Thirty years. A marsh
grows up around the house.
Schools of spores circulate
behind the shades, drift through
gauze flutterings of vegetation.

LOUISE GLÜCK

A Grief Beyond Remedy

Once again the machine breaks down. She kicks it
    twice.
No go. / Her mother stands over it, glaring
as if it were just one more unhandy daughter
she loves but can't live with. If only machines could
    listen.
It's all someone's fault. The damn thing wasn't brought
    up right,
was indulged or treated too strictly, not tenderly
    nurtured,

not taught to succeed. Someone blew out its motor
by overload, or left the front window open
till it sputtered and coughed and came down with the
    flu.

Once again the grown daughter is there in her mother's
    house,
a small child, helpless. Every morning she drags
    downstairs
to the doctor's prescribed menu that makes her gag.
She sulks and loses weight, nobody knows why.
Each day the stream of "suggestions" breaks surface at
    dawn,
forcing her downriver.
               Green is not her color.
  She should cut her hair short so people won't see that it's oily.
  She should put on a dress; jeans are for the country
  and the uncouth. Her homework is carelessly copied
    (appalled, she hears herself tell her young daughter
        this)
  her children ill-taught, her husband not kept in order
    (will she tell her daughter this too, ten years into
        the future?)
  her career tossed aside, her life put together stupidly,
  her furniture undusted, the wrong style, and badly arranged.
    (Is there no help for it, will all these things be true
    of her young child, as they may be true of her?
    when she speaks to her daughter, will her voice
        sound like this?)
  Not one of her daily machines to insure survival

can work. She should send them to the Thrift Shop and copy her
mother's.

She is not alone. There is nobody alive
or dead whose life her mother couldn't have planned
    and run better,
whose happiness her mother wouldn't have made good
    and sure of
had they all done everything other than what they did:

She knows it, this strong woman
who has worked for her family all her stubborn life,
who stood behind her husband like a rock that knew
    better,
upon whom all his work must constantly be beaten
    back
to run aground, to be shattered into wreckage, and then
    rebuilt
and sent out to sail, this time her own chosen craft,
her device, her machine, her ship, seaworthy and sure:

this strong woman
who tossed her own talent out for the laundry, the
    dishes,
the crafting of her children's minds, the tending of their
    talents,
the typing of her husband's letters, the work of keeping
the whole raft afloat as if they would sink without her,
as if they would even now, every single one,
sink to the bottom if she dared to let them alone:

this woman who drives them crazy and whom in the
        wreckage
                        they treat with forbearance,
as her young daughter forbears her now, in grief and
        anger,
as her mother forbears her now, in love and terror
                        as of a mirror
each time they touch
                        each time they touch.

                                        JUDITH JOHNSON

The Photos

My sister in her well-tailored silk blouse hands me
the photo of my father
in naval uniform and white hat.
I say, "Oh, this is the one which Mama used to have
        on her dresser."

My sister controls her face and furtively looks at my
        mother,
a sad rag bag of a woman, lumpy and sagging
        everywhere,
like a mattress at the Salvation Army, though with no
        holes or tears,
and says, "No."

I look again,
and see that my father is wearing a wedding ring,

which he never did
when he lived with my mother. And that there is a
    legend on it,
"To my dearest wife,
        Love
        Chief"
And I realize the photo must have belonged to his
    second wife,
whom he left our mother to marry.

My mother says, with her face as still as the whole
    unpopulated part of the state of North Dakota,
"May I see it too?"
She looks at it.

I look at my tailored sister
and my own blue-jeaned self. Have we wanted to hurt
    our mother,
sharing these pictures on this, one of the few days I
    ever visit or
spend with family? For her face is curiously haunted,
not now with her usual viperish bitterness,
but with something so deep it could not be spoken.

I turn away and say I must go on, as I have a dinner
    engagement with friends.
But I drive all the way to Pasadena from Whittier,
thinking of my mother's face; how I could never love
    her; how my father
could not love her either. Yet knowing I have
    inherited

the rag-bag body,
stony face with bulldog jaws.

I drive, thinking of that face.
Jeffers' California Medea who inspired me to poetry.
I killed my children,
but there as I am changing lanes on the freeway,
    necessarily glancing in the
rearview mirror, I see the face,
not even a ghost, but always with me, like a photo in a
    beloved's wallet.

How I hate my destiny.

DIANE WAKOSKI

Mother II

No one is "Woman" to another
woman, except her mother.
Her breasts were unmysterious
naked: limp, small. But I thought pus
must ooze from them: her underwear
like bandages. Blood came from where
I came from, stanched with pads between
her legs, under the girdle, seen
through gaping bathroom doors. Around
her waist, all sorts of rubber. Bound

to stop the milk, my milk, her breasts
stayed flat. I watched my round self, guessed
a future where I'd droop and leak.
But dry and cool against her cheek
I'd lean my cheek. I stroked the lace
and serge she sheathed her carapace
with: straight skirts, close cuffs, full sleeves;
was, wordless, catechized; believed:
nude, she was gaunt; dressed, she was slim;
nude, she was flabby; dressed, her firm
body matched her brisk, precise
mid-continental teacher's voice,
which she had molded, dry, perfect-
ed from a swamp of dialect.
Naked or clad, for me, she wore
her gender, perpetual *chador*,
her individual complex
history curtained off by sex.
Child, I determined that I would
not be subsumed in womanhood.
Whatever she was, I was not.
Whoever she was, I forgot
to ask, and she forgot to tell,
muffled in costumes she as well
rejected as a girl, resumed
—on my account? Are women doomed,
beasts that repeat ourselves, to rage
in youth against our own old age,
in age to circumscribe our youth
with self-despisal dressed as truth?

Am I "Woman" to my water-
dwelling brown loquacious daughter,
corporeal exemplar of
her thirst for what she would not love?

Why My Mother Made Me

Maybe I am what she always wanted,
my father as a woman,
maybe I am what she wanted to be
when she first saw him, tall and smart,
standing there in the college yard with the
hard male light of 1937
shining on his black hair. She wanted that
power. She wanted that size. She pulled and
pulled through him as if he were dark
bourbon taffy, she pulled and pulled and
pulled through his body until she drew me out,
rubbery and gleaming, her life after her life.
Maybe I am the way I am
because she wanted exactly that,
wanted there to be a woman
a lot like her, but who would not hold back, so she
pressed herself hard against him,
pressed and pressed the clear soft

ball of herself like a stick of beaten cream
against his stained sour steel grater
until I came out the other side of his body,
a big woman, stained, sour, sharp,
but with that milk at the center of my nature.
I lie here now as I once lay
in the crook of her arm, her creature,
and I feel her looking down into me the way the
maker of a sword gazes at his face in the
steel of the blade.

SHARON OLDS

Christmas Eve

Oh sharp diamond, my mother!
I could not count the cost
of all your faces, your moods—
that present that I lost.
Sweet girl, my deathbed,
my jewel-fingered lady,
your portrait flickered all night
by the bulbs of the tree.

Your face as calm as the moon
over a mannered sea,
presided at the family reunion,

the twelve grandchildren
you used to wear on your wrist,
a three-months-old baby,
a fat check you never wrote,
the red-haired toddler who danced the twist,
your aging daughters, each one a wife,
each one talking to the family cook,
each one avoiding your portrait,
each one aping your life.

Later, after the party,
after the house went to bed,
I sat up drinking the Christmas brandy,
watching your picture,
letting the tree move in and out of focus.
The bulbs vibrated.
They were a halo over your forehead.
Then they were a beehive,
blue, yellow, green, red;
each with its own juice, each hot and alive
stinging your face. But you did not move.
I continued to watch, forcing myself,
waiting, inexhaustible, thirty-five.

I wanted your eyes, like the shadows
of two small birds, to change.
But they did not age.
The smile that gathered me in, all wit,
all charm, was invincible.
Hour after hour I looked at your face

but I could not pull the roots out of it.
Then I watched how the sun hit
your red sweater, your withered neck,
your badly painted flesh-pink skin.
You who led me by the nose,
I saw you as you were.
Then I thought of your body
as one thinks of murder . . .

Then I said Mary—
Mary, Mary, forgive me
and then I touched a present for the child,
the last I bred before your death;
and then I touched my breast
and then I touched the floor
and then my breast again as if,
somehow, it were one of yours.

ANNE SEXTON

Heredity

My mother grows emaciated
in the Danish modern chair.

I have fattened past the dotted
limits of my assigned space, my cells,

my DNA, and forget I was ever afraid
to speak. My mother cannot finish

a sentence. I know how to unwind
her helices of tears. I know

which hairpin keeps her
from going haywire, know how far

I'd have to walk to put
unwooden arms around her, hug her

till the struts shook. When will I see
you again, she wonders, adjusting

her glasses. Don't mention
your father. Marry the man

of my dreams. Wear my bathrobe
with its yellow leashes. Let me

love you, need you,
know you, let me

go. The things we cannot say
slip buttered knives through the venetian blinds.

She cleans her glasses, says beneath
her breath the town is not the same. My tongue

goes over and over
its old home ground, in which, today, were fixed

these two new slick
white stones, my own

false teeth.

HEATHER McHUGH

Trinity Churchyard

For my mother & her ancestor, Akiba

Wherever I walked I went green among young
    growing
Along the same song, Mother, even along this grass
Where, Mother, tombstones stand each in its pail of
    shade
In Trinity yard where you at lunchtime came
As a young workingwoman, Mother, bunches of your
    days, grapes
Pressing your life into mine, Mother,

And I never cared for these tombs and graves
But they are your book-keeper hours.

You said to me summers later, deep in your shiniest
    car
As a different woman, Mother, and I your poem-
    making daughter—
"Each evening after I worked all day for the lock-
    people
"I wished under a green sky on the young evening
    star—
"What did I wish for?" What did you wish for,
    Mother?
"I wished for a man, of course, anywhere in my world,
"And there was Trinity graveyard and the tall New
    York steeples."

Wherever I go, Mother, I stay away from graves
But they turn everywhere in the turning world; now,
Mother Rachel's, on the road from Jerusalem.
And mine is somewhere turning unprepared
In the earth or among the whirling air.
My workingwoman mother is saying to me, Girl—
Years before her rich needy unreal years—
Whatever work you do, always make sure
You can go walking, not like me, shut in your hours.

Mother I walk, going even here in green Galilee
Where our ancestor, Akiba, resisted Rome,
Singing forever for the Song of Songs

Even in torture knowing.   Mother, I walk, this blue,
The Sea, Mother, this hillside, to his great white
    stone.
And again here in New York later I come alone
To you, Mother, I walk, making our poems.

MURIEL RUKEYSER

The Blessing

For Ashley

I.

Daughter-my-mother
you have observed my worst.
Holding me together at your expense
has made you burn cool.

So did I in childhood:
nursed her old hurts and doubts
myself made cool to shallowness.
She grew out as I grew in.
At mid-point, our furies met.

My mother's dust has rested
for fifteen years
in the front hall closet
because we couldn't bear to bury it.
Her dust-lined, dust-coated urn
squats among the size-eleven overshoes.
My father, who never forgets
his overshoes,
has forgotten that.

Hysterical-tongued daughter
of a dead marriage
you shed hot tears in the bed
of that benign old woman
whose fierce joy you were:
tantrums in the closet
taking upon yourself the guilt
the split parents never felt.

Child and old woman
soothing each other
sharing the same face
in a span of seventy years
the same mother wit.

I must go home, says my father,
his mind straying;
*this is a hard time
for your mother.* But she's been dead
these fifteen years.
Daughter and daughter, we sit

on either side.
Whose? Which? He's not sure.
After long silence
don't press me, he says.

II.

Mother, hysterical-tongued,
age and grace burned away
your excesses, left
that lavender-sweet child
who turned up the thermostat
on her electric blanket, folded
her hands on her breast;
you had dreamed death
as a silver prince:
like marrying Nehru, you said.

Dearest, does your dust hum
in the front hall closet
this is a hard time for me
among the umbrella points
the canes and overshoes
of that cold climate?

Each week she denies it
my blithe mother
in that green, cloud-free landscape
where we whisper our dream-secrets
to each other.

III.

Daughter, you lived through
my difficult affairs
as I tried to console
your burnt-out childhood.
We coped with our fathers
compared notes
on the old one and the cold one,
learned to moderate our hates.
Risible in suffering
we grew up together.

Mother-my-daughter
I have been blessed
on both sides of my life.
Forgive me if sometimes
like my fading father
I see you as one.

Not that I confuse
your two identities
as he does, taking off
or putting on his overshoes,
but my own role:

I lean on the bosom
of that double mother
the ghost by night, the girl by day,
I between my

two mild furies
alone but comforted.

And I will whisper blithely
in your dreams
when you are as old as I
my hard time over.
Meanwhile, keep warm
your love, your bed
and your wise heart and head
my good daughter.

CAROLYN KIZER

VII

To My First Love: Celebrating the Mother

$\mathcal{F}$or most of us, love is the lesson of the mother's breast, and most of us, luckily, continue to be educated by maternal love throughout childhood. How to live, how to love, and even how to learn—these are lore taught by the mother, through example perhaps even more than through direct statement. No wonder that the mother is almost every child's first love, first heroine. Her "heart is my heart's quiet home," confesses Christina Rossetti while Rudyard Kipling confides, "If I were damned of body and soul,/I know whose prayers would make me whole," and Edna St. Vincent Millay longs for "the courage that my mother had." Sometimes indeed the beloved mother seems so powerful that she's a little larger than life and more than a bit magical. "They were women then/My mama's generation," marvels Alice Walker, and Richard Garcia dreams "the stars shining in my mother's hair." "If there are any heavens," muses the ordinarily skeptical E. E. Cummings, "my mother will(all by herself)have/one."

if there are any heavens my mother
will(all by herself)have

if there are any heavens my mother will(all by herself)
    have
one.   It will not be a pansy heaven nor
a fragile heaven of lilies-of-the-valley but
it will be a heaven of blackred roses

my father will be(deep like a rose
tall like a rose)

standing near my

(swaying over her
silent)
with eyes which are really petals and see

nothing with the face of a poet really which
is a flower and not a face with
hands
which whisper
This is my beloved my

                    (suddenly in sunlight
he will bow,

& the whole garden will bow)

E. E. CUMMINGS

Mother o' Mine

If I were hanged on the highest hill,
Mother o' mine, O mother o' mine!
I know whose love would follow me still,
Mother o' mine, O mother o' mine!

If I were drowned in the deepest sea,
Mother o' mine, O mother o' mine!
I know whose tears would come down to me,
Mother o' mine, O mother o' mine!

If I were damned of body and soul,
I know whose prayers would make me whole,
Mother o' mine, O mother o' mine!

RUDYARD KIPLING

The courage that my mother had

The courage that my mother had
Went with her, and is with her still:
Rock from New England quarried;
Now granite in a granite hill.

The golden brooch my mother wore
She left behind for me to wear;

I have no thing I treasure more:
Yet, it is something I could spare.

Oh, if instead she'd left to me
The thing she took into the grave!—
That courage like a rock, which she
Has no more need of, and I have.

EDNA ST. VINCENT MILLAY

Women

They were women then
My mama's generation
Husky of voice—Stout of
Step
With fists as well as
Hands
How they battered down
Doors
And ironed
Starched white
Shirts
How they led
Armies
Headragged Generals
Across mined

Fields
Booby-trapped
Ditches
To discover books
Desks
A place for us
How they knew what we
Must know
Without knowing a page
Of it
Themselves.

ALICE WALKER

The Adversary

A mother's hardest to forgive.
Life is the fruit she longs to hand you,
Ripe on a plate. And while you live,
Relentlessly she understands you.

PHYLLIS McGINLEY

My Mother in Three Acts

At the top of the hill you were Muriel,
pale but still powerful as a Sumo wrestler,
generous, mother of mysteries held in reserve.
You were already dead then; I knew I couldn't save you.
In the nursery school room I began to rearrange
brightly colored clay figures: *la Sagrada Familia.*

Tripping down the hill you were Betty,
blond and still fashionable but too thin,
needling me, cosseting me. Dying of cancer
only sharpened your wit. I knew I couldn't save you—
I could barely even keep up! Mother of the quick retort,
of the enchanting story, mother of gifts and
     dissatisfactions.

At the bottom of the hill just as we reached the
house I had rented, I glimpsed a fugitive girl,
face turned aside toward the woods, slipping away
in a seagreen Japanese kimono; her hair was brown.
Was it you, mother of boyishness, mother of
deception, who saved me once, the one who evades me
     still?

JANE COOPER

My Mama moved among the days

My Mama moved among the days
like a dreamwalker in a field;
seemed like what she touched was hers
seemed like what touched her couldn't hold,
she got us almost through the high grass
then seemed like she turned around and ran
right back in
right back on in

LUCILLE CLIFTON

In the Ocean

At first my mother would be shy
Leaving my lame father behind

But then she would tuck up her bathing cap
And fly into the water like a dolphin,

Slippery as bamboo she would bend
Everywhere, everywhere I remember

For though he would often be criticizing her,
Blaming her, finding fault

Behind her back he would talk about her
All through our childhood, to me and my sister,

She rarely spoke against him

Except to take us by the hand
In the ocean we would laugh together

As we never did, on dry land

Because he was an invalid
Usually she was silent

But this once, on her deathbed

Hearing me tell it she remembered
Almost before I did, and she smiled

One more time to think of it,
How, with the waves crashing at our feet

Slithering all over her wet skin

We would rub against her like minnows
We would flow between her legs, in the surf

Smooth as spaghetti she would hold us
Close against her like small polliwogs climbing

All over her as if she were a hill,
A hill that moved, our element

But hers also, safe
In the oval of each other's arms

This once she would be weightless
As guiltless, utterly free

Of all but what she loved
Smoothly, with no hard edges,

My long beautiful mother
In her white bathing cap, crowned

Like an enormous lily

Over the brown arrow of her body,
The limber poles of her legs,

The sad slanted eyes,
The strong cheekbones, and the shadows

Like fluid lavender, everywhere

Looping and sliding through the waves
We would swim together as one

In a rainbow of breaking foam

Mother and sea calves gliding,
Floating as if all three of us were flying.

PATRICIA GOEDICKE

The Mother Before Memory

1.

Enormous mythic figures shine in a silent dark,
the mother with child at her breast, her knee.

Photographs flash past like an art history
lecture, but with no blue-cloaked white Virgin,

no black vulture-winged, horn-crowned Isis
hiding the tiny boy god.   Instead there I am,
the child, ringletted, lace-collar smock, white
on white skin, leaning against the black mother,
massive, enigmatic, weighty hat, dark clothes.
Both stare unsmiling at the camera.   Who paid
for this picture?   What did they want remembered?

Long years after, what does the child think,
looking at the picture?   In my hands it would bend:
soft pasteboard, sepia, antique, shocking
proof of time when it was us only, the two of us.
(Does the child say *my black mother?*) I have a picture
of her holding me in her arms, up in the sunlight.
She is in headrag and sagging apron.   The backyard,
the scuppernong vine shadow.   1946.   I am a baby.
It is a breath of time in the years she held me.

2.

Pictures somewhere, in a cardboard candy box,
my mother holding me.   (Does the child say
my white mother?) What I remember is a story:
how those years before memory I never cried.
She squatted by me, tried an even, reasoned voice.
I never cried.   No memory of her mouth, her face.

I remember lying by her, massive in the dark,
the slow beating of her voice through hymns,
through last century's love songs, and I slept.

I remember her proud silence.   But somewhere
her voice talks to her self in me.   Somewhere
in me a voice like our church bell that rang
once a week only: the harsh repeated metal clang,
outcry in silence.   Her voice praying in me.

MINNIE BRUCE PRATT

Dear Mama (4)

when did we become friends?
it happened so gradual i didn't notice
maybe i had to get my run out first
take a big bite of the honky world and choke on it
maybe that's what has to happen with some uppity
     youngsters
if it happens at all

and now
the thought stark and irrevocable
of being here without you
shakes me

beyond love, fear, regret or anger
into that realm children go
who want to care for/protect their parents
as if they could
and sometimes the lucky ones do

into the realm of making every moment
important
laughing as though laughter wards off death
each word given
received like spanish eight

treasure to bury within
against that shadow day
when it will be the only coin i possess
with which to buy peace of mind

WANDA COLEMAN

My mother was a braid of black smoke

My mother was a braid of black smoke.
She bore me swaddled over the burning cities.
The sky was a vast and windy place for a child to
play.

We met many others who were just like us. They
were trying to put on their overcoats with arms made of
smoke,

The high heavens were full of little shrunken deaf
ears instead of stars.

CHARLES SIMIC

A Poem for Sarah's Mother

"My mother was a widow. She cleaned offices.
She sent all four of us to college."—Student theme

Those evenings the offices are cold; the chill gets in
    under your ears,
Sends an iron bar from here to here; I imagine her
Like a kind of saint hassling a dragon, a prophetess,
Toes locked against an angel on the edge of a cliff,
The angel says, prove; it says, behave.
It says, one night on a cliff is fine; afterwards
They go away, they turn your hopes inside out.
No one will remember a thing about you and your
    mop.

One of those fighters had to go over; one
Had to stand on its forehead in the chasm, bat hair
    flying.
Fall like my wishes, the mother said.
Your arms wrenched back into broken wings,
Angel. I'll wallop it out of you.

The mother is tall, her hair tied behind her ears in a
    kerchief.
The worst part of her day is midnight:
The tiredness of soup, sullen radio,
Sleeping children, the angel who follows after, wings
    akimbo,

Edges of feather dipped in paint. It has a neon line
    around it. It says,
I'll wrestle with you, lady.

My student thinks herself an ordinary woman
Except for that battle. That's one of those childhood
    flashes
That startles sleep, that lights up Oakland afterward.
She says: They fought. The angel glowed like an electric
    heating element.
They fought for fifteen years.
My mother won.

DIANA O'HEHIR

In an Iridescent Time

My mother, when young, scrubbed laundry in a tub,
She and her sisters on an old brick walk
Under the apple trees, sweet rub-a-dub.
The bees came round their heads, the wrens made talk.
Four young ladies each with a rainbow board
Honed their knuckles, wrung their wrists to red,
Tossed back their braids and wiped their aprons wet.
The Jersey calf beyond the back fence roared;
And all the soft day, swarms about their pet
Buzzed at his big brown eyes and bullish head.

Four times they rinsed, they said. Some things they
      starched,
Then shook them from the baskets two by two,
And pinned the fluttering intimacies of life
Between the lilac bushes and the yew:
Brown gingham, pink, and skirts of Alice blue.

RUTH STONE

From the House of Yemanjá

My mother had two faces and a frying pot
where she cooked up her daughters
into girls
before she fixed our dinner.
My mother had two faces
and a broken pot
where she hid out a perfect daughter
who was not me
I am the sun and moon and forever hungry
for her eyes.

I bear two women upon my back
one dark and rich and hidden
in the ivory hungers of the other
mother
pale as a witch
yet steady and familiar

brings me bread and terror
in my sleep
her breasts are huge exciting anchors
in the midnight storm.

All this has been
before
in my mother's bed
time has no sense
I have no brothers
and my sisters are cruel.

Mother I need
mother I need
mother I need your blackness now
as the august earth needs rain.
I am
the sun and moon and forever hungry
the sharpened edge
where day and night shall meet
and not be
one.

AUDRE LORDE

Sonnets are full of love,
and this my tome

Sonnets are full of love, and this my tome
    Has many sonnets: so here now shall be
    One sonnet more, a love sonnet, from me
To her whose heart is my heart's quiet home,
    To my first Love, my Mother, on whose knee
I learnt love-lore that is not troublesome;
    Whose service is my special dignity,
And she my loadstar while I go and come.
And so because you love me, and because
    I love you, Mother, I have woven a wreath
        Of rhymes wherewith to crown your honoured
            name:
        In you not fourscore years can dim the flame
Of love, whose blessed glow transcends the laws
    Of time and change and mortal life and death.

CHRISTINA ROSSETTI

Mi Mamá, the Playgirl

    When my mother left Mexico, soldiers comman-
deered the train, forcing the passengers to get off and
wait for the next one. Later they passed it lying on its
side, burning.

She wore black dresses. Her closet was lined with identical pairs of black shoes. She constantly advised me to jump off the bridge while the tide was going out.

Long after my father was dead, she complained that his side of the bed still sank down. *"Viejo,"* she would tell him, "if you have somewhere to go, please go." At seventy, she went out to nightclubs. Twisted her knee doing the bunny hop. Talked for hours to forty-year-old lovers on the phone. My brothers were ashamed.

After she died, she came to see me as she had promised. My father came, too. We sat around in the kitchen drinking coffee as if nothing had happened. My father looked great, said he'd been working out. She stroked his forearm, smiling at his tattoo of the dancing hula girl. When they left it was nothing dramatic. They just walked out the door and up a street that seemed to reach into the night sky. How beautiful, I thought, as I was waking, the stars shining in my mother's hair.

RICHARD GARCIA

VIII

SILVER THREADS:
THE AGING MOTHER

*I*t's a frightening time, the season of watching that one who once was all-powerful become weaker, pack up, prepare to leave.

The children who observe their aging mothers in this section's poems are asking a series of unspoken questions: Why are you leaving? How does it feel? Was it worth it? Why so physical? Will it happen to me, too?

Most of the mothers don't answer; the ones who speak out offer vigorous agendas of their own. Pearl Bond's Jewish mother in the poem of the same name says, "I will dance at your wedding/in spite of gout & 200 pounds"; in Tess Gallagher's poem ". . . the beautiful one speaks to me from the changed, proud face . . ." ("My Mother Remembers That She Was Beautiful").

In this section, children once again regard their mothers with combined affection, fear, and alarm, sensing reiteration in their own futures of the experience they are watching. And once again mothers are angled in a different direction. In Denise Levertov's poem "The 90th Year," the dying mother writes to her daughter, " 'I am so tired . . . of appreciating the gift of life.' "

The old face of the mother of many children

The old face of the mother of many children,
Whist! I am fully content.

Lull'd and late is the smoke of the First-day morning,
It hangs low over the rows of trees by the fences,
It hangs thin by the sassafras and wild-cherry and cat-
  brier under them.

I saw the rich ladies in full dress at the soiree,
I heard what the singers were singing so long,
Heard who sprang in crimson youth from the white
  froth and the water-blue.

Behold a woman!
She looks out from her quaker cap, her face is clearer
  and more beautiful than the sky.

She sits in an armchair under the shaded porch of the
  farmhouse,
The sun just shines on her old white head.

Her ample gown is of cream-hued linen,
Her grandsons raised the flax, and her grand-daughters
  spun it with the distaff and the wheel.

The melodious character of the earth,
The finish beyond which philosophy cannot go and
    does not wish to go,
The justified mother of men.

WALT WHITMAN

Last Will

Children,
when I am ash
read by the light of the fire
that consumes me
this document
whose subject is love.

I want to leave you everything: my life
divided into so many parts
there are enough to go around; the world
from this window: weather and a tree
which bequeaths
all of its leaves each year.

Today the lawyer plans
for your descendants,
telling a story
of generations
that seems to come true
even as he speaks.

My books will fill
your children's shelves,
my small enameled spoons
invade their drawers. It is
the only way I know, so far,
to haunt.

Let me be a guest at my own funeral
and at the reading of my will.
You I'll reward first
for the moments of your births,
those three brief instants
when I understood my life.

But wisdom bends as light does
around the objects it touches.
The only legacy you need was left
by accident long ago:
a secret in the genes.
The rest is small change.

LINDA PASTAN

My Mother Remembers That She Was Beautiful

For Georgia Morris Bond

The falling snow has made her thoughtful
and young in the privacy
of our table with its netted candle
and thick white plates. The serious faces
of the lights breathe on the pine boards
behind her. She is visiting
the daughter never close
or far enough away to come to.

She keeps her coat on, called into
her girlhood by such forgetting
I am gone or yet
to happen. She sees herself
among the townspeople, the country glances
slow with fields and sky
as she passes or waits
with a brother in the hot animal smell
of the auction stand: sunlight,
straw hats, a dog's tail
brushing her bare leg.

"There are things you know.
I didn't have to beg," she said, "for anything."

The beautiful one speaks to me
from the changed, proud face and I see

how little I've let her know
of what she becomes. Years
were never the trouble, or the white hair
I braided near the sea
on a summer day. Who
she must have been
is lost to me through some fault
in my own reflection and we will have to go on
as we think we are, walking for no one's sake
from the empty restaurant into the one color
of the snow—before us, the close houses,
the brave and wondering lights of the houses.

TESS GALLAGHER

Eightythree

My mother sits on a towel
on the toilet seat. I dip a cloth
into lukewarm suds and wash her face and neck,
her dry, crevassed neck.

She says, "Sometimes I feel as dark and alone
as before I was born."

I wash her arms, her elbows, the crooks of her elbows,
her underarms.

"That feels good," she says.

I wash her back round and fleshy, the tired
breasts, her belly broad and generous as an old
Renoir. I wash her buttocks, those large apples,
so like my own.

She says, "I'm no good for anybody,
not even for myself."

I wash her thighs and knees, her gnarled toes,
pat her dry, rub her all over with oil.

She says, "Am I your baby?"

Ruth Whitman

The 90th Year

High in the jacaranda shines the gilded thread
of a small bird's curlicue of song—too high
for her to see or hear.
                          I've learned
not to say, these last years,
"O, look!—O listen, Mother!"
as I used to.
                    (It was she
who taught me to look;
to name the flowers when I was still close to the
    ground,
my face level with theirs;

or to watch the sublime metamorphoses
unfold and unfold
over the walled back gardens of our street . . .

It had not been given her
to know the flesh as good in itself,
as the flesh of a fruit is good. To her
the human body has been a husk,
a shell in which souls were prisoned.
Yet, from within it, with how much gazing
her life has paid tribute to the world's body!
How tears of pleasure
would choke her, when a perfect voice,
deep or high, clove to its note unfaltering!)

She has swept the crackling seedpots,
the litter of mauve blossoms, off the cement path,
tipped them into the rubbish bucket.
She's made her bed, washed up the breakfast dishes,
wiped the hotplate. I've taken the butter and milkjug
back to the fridge next door—but it's not my place,
visiting here, to usurp the tasks
that weave the day's pattern.
Now she is leaning forward in her chair,
                    by the lamp lit in the daylight,
rereading *War and Peace.*
                    When I look up
from her wellworn copy of *The Divine Milieu,*
which she wants me to read, I see her hand
loose on the black stem of the magnifying glass,

she is dozing.
"I am so tired," she has written to me, "of appreciating
the gift of life."

DENISE LEVERTOV

The Song of the Old Mother

I rise in the dawn, and I kneel and blow
Till the seed of the fire flicker and glow;
And then I must scrub and bake and sweep
Till stars are beginning to blink and peep;
And the young lie long and dream in their bed
Of the matching of ribbons for bosom and head,
And their day goes over in idleness,
And they sigh if the wind but lift a tress:
While I must work because I am old,
And the seed of the fire gets feeble and cold.

WILLIAM BUTLER YEATS

The Youngest Daughter

The sky has been dark
for many years.
My skin has become as damp
and pale as rice paper
and feels the way
mother's used to before the drying sun
parched it out there in the fields.

       Lately, when I touch my eyelids,
my hands react as if
I had just touched something
hot enough to burn.
My skin, aspirin colored,
tingles with migraine. Mother
has been massaging the left side of my face
especially in the evenings
when the pain flares up.

This morning
her breathing was graveled,
her voice gruff with affection
when I wheeled her into the bath.
She was in a good humor,
making jokes about her great breasts,
floating in the milky water
like two walruses,
flaccid and whiskered around the nipples.
I scrubbed them with a sour taste
in my mouth, thinking:

six children and an old man
have sucked from these brown nipples.

I was almost tender
when I came to the blue bruises
that freckle her body,
places where she has been injecting insulin
for thirty years. I soaped her slowly,
she sighed deeply, her eyes closed.
It seems it has always
been like this: the two of us
in this sunless room,
the splashing of the bathwater.

In the afternoons
when she has rested,
she prepares our ritual of tea and rice,
garnished with a shred of gingered fish,
a slice of pickled turnip,
a token for my white body.
We eat in the familiar silence.
She knows I am not to be trusted,
even now planning my escape.
As I toast to her health
with the tea she has poured,
a thousand cranes curtain the window,
fly up in a sudden breeze.

CATHY SONG

Jewish Mother

For Della

I will dance at your wedding
in spite of gout & 200 lbs.
Indian fakirs walk on
nails in their ecstasy.
Daughter this tradition
is in my blood;
it cannot be a stately dance.
my pendulous anatomy will
defy gravity, though you play
rock music I will hear
the Russian Kazatsky
wild & beating in my eardrums
I shall leap like the Slavic
bear in rippling girth,
the world & the moment
may pass in review—
my love will sustain me;
should I die before you marry,
I pledge my honor to dance
at your wedding, I will come
from eons, frost & stars
you will hear violins & tambourines
radiance will be your destiny.

PEARL BOND

Nursing: Mother

1

Tranquilized, she speaks or does not speak;
Immobilized, she goes to & fro invisibly.
The names of my children she recalls
Like a declension; my ex-husband is,
She thinks, the verb of a bad dream she had,
Irregular. When she listens,
What does she hear?
Kept in so long after school, it is her wits
That she, old traveller, sends wandering.
                                        What joke
Will make her laugh? Doctor
Is she in pain? To her the nurse
Talks loud & slow as to a foreigner;
To whom have age and injury made
This most local woman alien?

Patient, she lies like a paradigm
Elaborate on her fenced high bed because
Her hip-bone snapped. Her doctor
Indicates his neat repair. I flinch
Before her sacredness.

From between those thighs
(Splashed in those days iridescent
With brigher-than-blood mercurochrome)
I thrust into sight thirsting for air

(So it must have been; so my children came;
So we commit by embodying it, woman to woman,
Our power: to set life free.
She set me free).

———◆———

Long closed against me, now her flesh
Is a text I guess to read: Is
She in pain? My own flesh aches dumb
For a mummer's gift of touch
We might use to speak ourselves
Against this last fitful light
To mime the thirst we have.

2

To visit her I go among the graduates
Of ordinary discourse, where wryly
They command them who keep them.
Where they live is hot, rank, preserved,
Lion country.

In state among them Mother
Has her Lying-In as
Infant Empress whose otherness
Confuses the lions
And instructs them tame.

Where I dream she still walks domestic
In a peacock dress, bead-embroidered,
Aloof among my garden's raucous goats.

I dream her as blessing, with birds as gifts;
I dream her as the Tower's Priestess of cruel
Removal and Return, stepping in & out
At her will of her warm shadow, me.
I dream her serene, regent in her own
Diamonded mystery.

———◆———

If I am hers she does not feel it.
The Empress Infant has no child.
She watches their antics as if her look
Kept the subject lions staked and tethered
Where they stalk. But suddenly,
"To see you," she says, "brightens me."

3

Here or dream, she is not at home. She
Can only come home to a boxroom brownstone
For breakfast on fried oysters & talk of the news
Of ships' arrivals in the Sunday *Tribune*
Between a man and woman who love her;
And even the walls of her homing are
Dust these forty years.

What she has kept of who she is
Is what the part calls for: a
Winsome dominance, speaking up
With a half-lost sense of audience; do
They tire of her she sleeps; do they smile
She is glad of it; what is she practicing?

Here on the flat of her bed the size
Of a flat box already ready in a factory.

Empress and Infant fear the toppling of the Tower.
She wishes the visitor were her mother, but
Trying it, saying, "Mom! How's Pop?"
Quickly adds, "Never mind. Never mind."

———◆———

Today she said, "In the sun
Your hair has many colors,"
Quickly adding, "With these glasses
You got me, of course, I'm nearly blind."

                                MARIE PONSOT

Soloing

My mother tells me she dreamed
of John Coltrane, a young Trane
playing his music with such joy
and contained energy and rage
she could not hold back her tears.
And sitting awake now, her hands
crossed in her lap, the tears start
in her blind eyes. The TV set
behind her is gray, expressionless.
It is late, the neighbors quiet,
even the city—Los Angeles—quiet.
I have driven for hours down 99,
over the Grapevine into heaven
to be here. I place my left hand
on her shoulder, and she smiles.
What a world, a mother and son
finding solace in California
just where we were told it would
be, among the palm trees and all-
night super markets pushing orange
back-lighted oranges at 2 A.M.
"He was alone," she says, and does
not say, just as I am, "soloing."
What a world, a great man half
her age comes to my mother
in sleep to give her the gift
of song, which—shaking the tears

234

away—she passes on to me, for now
I can hear the music of the world
in the silence and that word:
soloing. What a world—when I
arrived the great bowl of mountains
was hidden in a cloud of exhaust,
the sea spread out like a carpet
of oil, the roses I had brought
from Fresno browned on the seat
beside me, and I could have
turned back and lost the music.

PHILIP LEVINE

Lucinda Matlock

I went to the dances at Chandlerville,
And played snap-out at Winchester.
One time we changed partners,
Driving home in the moonlight of middle June,
And then I found Davis.
We were married and lived together for seventy years,
Enjoying, working, raising the twelve children,
Eight of whom we lost
Ere I had reached the age of sixty.
I spun, I wove, I kept the house, I nursed the sick,
I made the garden, and for holiday

Rambled over the fields where sang the larks,
And by Spoon River gathering many a shell,
And many a flower and medicinal weed—
Shouting to the wooded hills, singing to the green
    valleys.
At ninety-six I had lived enough, that is all,
And passed to a sweet repose.
What is this I hear of sorrow and weariness,
Anger, discontent and drooping hopes?
Degenerate sons and daughters,
Life is too strong for you—
It takes life to love Life.

EDGAR LEE MASTERS

The Song of Absinthe Granny

Among some hills there dwelt in parody
A young woman; me.
I was that gone with child
That before I knew it I had three
And they hung whining and twisting.
Why I wasn't more than thirty-nine
And sparse as a runt fruit tree.
Three pips that plagued the life out of me.
Ah me. It wore me down,
The grubs, the grubbing.

We were two inches thick in dust
For lack of scrubbing.
Diapers and panty-shirts and yolk of eggs.
One day in the mirror I saw my stringy legs
And I looked around
And saw string on the floor,
And string on the chair
And heads like wasps' nests
Full of stringy hair.
"Well," I said, "if you have string, knit.
Knit something, don't just sit."
We had the orchard drops,
But they didn't keep.
The milk came in bottles.
It came until the bottles were that deep
We fell over the bottles.
The milk dried on the floor.
"Drink it up," cried their papa,
And they all began to roar, "More!"
Well, time went on,
Not a bone that wasn't frayed.
Every chit was knicked and bit,
And nothing was paid.
We had the dog spayed.
"It looks like a lifetime,"
Their papa said.

"It's a good life, it's a good wife,
It's a good bed."
So I got the rifle out

To shoot him through the head.
But he went on smiling and sitting
And I looked around for a piece of string
To do some knitting.
Then I picked at the tiling
And the house fell down.
"Now you've done it," he said.
"I'm going to town.
Get them up out of there,
Put them to bed."
"I'm afraid to look," I whimpered,
"They might be dead."
"We're here, Mama, under the shed."
Well, the winters wore on.
We had cats that hung around.
When I fed them they scratched.
How the little nippers loved them.
Cats and brats.
I couldn't see for my head was thatched
But they kept coming in when the door unlatched.
"I'll shave my head," I promised,
"I'll clip my mop.
This caterwauling has got to stop."
Well, all that's finished,
It's all been done.
Those were high kick summers,
It was bald galled fun.
Now the daft time's over
And the string is spun.
I'm all alone

To cull and be furry.
Not an extra page in the spanking story.
The wet britches dried
And the teeth came in.
The last one cried
And no new began.
Those were long hot summers,
Now the sun won't tarry.
My birds have flocked,
And I'm old and wary.
I'm old and worn and a cunning sipper,
And I'll outlive every little nipper.
And with what's left I'm chary,
And with what's left I'm chary.

RUTH STONE

IX

My Grandmothers
Were Strong:
Exploring Origins

Our part title here comes from Margaret Walker's wistful tribute to the sturdiness of her grandmothers and her worry that she cannot measure up to their standards. Praise songs to the past as well as apprehensions about the future combine in many poems dedicated to grandmothers. "I remember," Kathleen Raine promises over and over again, just as Hart Crane describes "how much room for memory there is" and Karl Shapiro equates his grandmother's evolution with "history [that] moved her through/Stranger lands and many houses." Understandably, then, Thomas Hardy sees the grandmother as the very principle of memory, for "past things retold were to her as things existent."

Precisely the evocative otherness of the grandmother enhances her magic for the poets represented here. Though the words of grandmothers do not always make immediate sense to the young, they hang resonant in the air, full of strange promise. Carolyn Forché's grandmother tells "filthy stories about the blood sausage" in "Slovak"; Elizabeth Bishop's "sings to the marvellous stove"; C. D. Wright's enigmatically asserts "Even. If. The. Sky. Is. Falling./My. Peace. Rose. Is. In. Bloom"; and Judith Ortiz Cofer's warns each of her daughters that "*children are made in the night and/steal your days/for the rest of your life, amen.*" To the grandchild who would be a poet, such mysterious figures are particularly inspiring.

Lineage

My grandmothers were strong.
They followed plows and bent to toil.
They moved through fields sowing seed.

They touched earth and grain grew.
They were full of sturdiness and singing.
My grandmothers were strong.

My grandmothers are full of memories
Smelling of soap and onions and wet clay
With veins rolling roughly over quick hands
They have many clean words to say.
My grandmothers were strong.
Why am I not as they?

MARGARET WALKER

Grandmother

Out of her own body she pushed
silver thread, light, air
and carried it carefully on the dark, flying
where nothing moved.

Out of her body she extruded
shining wire, life, and wove the light
on the void.

From beyond time,
beyond oak trees and bright clear water flow,
she was given the work of weaving the strands
of her body, her pain, her vision
into creation, and the gift of having created,
to disappear.

After her,
the women and the men weave blankets into tales of
     life,
memories of light and ladders,
infinity-eyes, and rain.
After her I sit on my laddered rain-bearing rug
and mend the tear with string.

PAULA GUNN ALLEN

The Morning Baking

Grandma, come back, I forgot
How much lard for these rolls

Think you can put yourself in the ground
Like plain potatoes and grow in Ohio?
I am damn sick of getting fat like you

Think you can lie through your Slovak?
Tell filthy stories about the blood sausage?
Pish-pish nights at the virgin in Detroit?

I blame your raising me up for my Slav tongue
You beat me up out back, taught me to dance

I'll tell you I don't remember any kind of bread
Your wavy loaves of flesh
Stink through my sleep
The stars on your silk robes

But I'm glad I'll look when I'm old
Like a gypsy dusha hauling milk

CAROLYN FORCHÉ

Sestina

September rain falls on the house.
In the failing light, the old grandmother
sits in the kitchen with the child
beside the Little Marvel Stove,
reading the jokes from the almanac,
laughing and talking to hide her tears.

She thinks that her equinoctial tears
and the rain that beats on the roof of the house
were both foretold by the almanac,

but only known to a grandmother.
The iron kettle sings on the stove.
She cuts some bread and says to the child,

It's time for tea now; but the child
is watching the teakettle's small hard tears
dance like mad on the hot black stove,
the way the rain must dance on the house.
Tidying up, the old grandmother
hangs up the clever almanac

on its string. Birdlike, the almanac
hovers half open above the child,
hovers above the old grandmother
and her teacup full of dark brown tears.
She shivers and says she thinks the house
feels chilly, and puts more wood in the stove.

It was to be, says the Marvel Stove.
I know what I know, says the almanac.
With crayons the child draws a rigid house
and winding pathway. Then the child
puts in a man with buttons like tears
and shows it proudly to the grandmother.

But secretly, while the grandmother
busies herself about the stove,
the little moons fall down like tears
from between the pages of the almanac
into the flower bed the child
has carefully placed in the front of the house.

Time to plant tears, says the almanac.
The grandmother sings to the marvellous stove
and the child draws another inscrutable house.

ELIZABETH BISHOP

My Grandmother

My grandmother moves to my mind in context of
    sorrow
And, as if apprehensive of near death, in black;
Whether erect in chair, her dry and corded throat
    harangued by grief,
Or at ragged book bent in Hebrew prayer,
Or gentle, submissive, and in tears to strangers;
Whether in sunny parlor or back of drawn blinds.

Though time and tongue made any love disparate,
On daguerreotype with classic perspective
Beauty I sigh and soften at is hers.
I pity her life of deaths, the agony of her own,
But most that history moved her through
Stranger lands and many houses,
Taking her exile for granted, confusing
The tongues and tasks of her children's children.

KARL SHAPIRO

The Last Words of My English Grandmother

There were some dirty plates
and a glass of milk
beside her on a small table
near the rank, disheveled bed—

Wrinkled and nearly blind
she lay and snored
rousing with anger in her tones
to cry for food,

Gimme something to eat—
They're starving me—
I'm all right—I won't go
to the hospital. No, no, no

Give me something to eat!
Let me take you
to the hospital, I said
and after you are well

you can do as you please.
She smiled, Yes
you do what you please first
then I can do what I please—

Oh, oh, oh! she cried
as the ambulance men lifted

her to the stretcher—
Is this what you call

making me comfortable?
By now her mind was clear—
Oh you think you're smart
you young people,

she said, but I'll tell you
you don't know anything.
Then we started.
On the way

we passed a long row
of elms, she looked at them
awhile out of
the ambulance window and said,

What are all those
fuzzy looking things out there?
Trees? Well, I'm tired
of them and rolled her head away.

WILLIAM CARLOS WILLIAMS

More Blues and the Abstract Truth

I back the car over a soft, large object;
hair appears on my chest in dreams.
The paper boy comes to collect
with a pitbull. Call Grandmother
and she says, Well you know
death is death and none other.

In the mornings we're in the dark;
even at the end of June
the zucchini keep on the sill.
Ring Grandmother for advice
and she says, O you know
I used to grow so many things.

Then there's the frequent bleeding,
the tender nipples and the rot
under the floormat. If I'm not seeing
a cold-eyed doctor it is
another gouging mechanic.
Grandmother says, Thanks to the blue rugs
and Eileen Briscoe's elms
the house keeps cool.

Well. Then. You say Grandmother
let me just ask you this:
How does a body rise again and rinse
her mouth from the tap. And how

does a body put in a plum tree
or lie again on top of another body
or string a trellis. Or go on drying
the flatware. Fix rainbow trout. Grout the tile.

Buy a bag of onions. Beat an egg stiff. Yes,
how does the cat continue
to lick itself from toenail to tailhole.
And how does a body break
bread with the word when the word
has broken. Again. And. Again.
With the wine. And the loaf.
And the excellent glass
of the body. And she says,

Even. If. The. Sky. Is. Falling.
My. Peace. Rose. Is. In. Bloom.

C. D. WRIGHT

My Grandmother's Love Letters

There are no stars to-night
But those of memory.
Yet how much room for memory there is
In the loose girdle of soft rain.

There is even room enough
For the letters of my mother's mother,
Elizabeth,
That have been pressed so long
Into a corner of the roof
That they are brown and soft,
And liable to melt as snow.

Over the greatness of such space
Steps must be gentle.
It is all hung by an invisible white hair.
It trembles as birch limbs webbing the air.

And I ask myself:

"Are your fingers long enough to play
Old keys that are but echoes:
Is the silence strong enough
To carry back the music to its source
And back to you again
As though to her?"

Yet I would lead my grandmother by the hand
Through much of what she would not understand;
And so I stumble. And the rain continues on the roof
With such a sound of gently pitying laughter.

HART CRANE

Green Rain

I remember long veils of green rain
Feathered like the shawl of my grandmother—
Green from the half-green of the spring trees
Waving in the valley.

I remember the road
Like the one which leads to my grandmother's house,
A warm house, with green carpets,
Geraniums, a trilling canary
And shining horse-hair chairs;
And the silence, full of the rain's falling
Was like my grandmother's parlour
Alive with herself and her voice, rising and falling—
Rain and wind intermingled.

I remember on that day
I was thinking only of my love
And of my love's house.
But now I remember the day
As I remember my grandmother.
I remember the rain as the feathery fringe of her shawl.

DOROTHY LIVESAY

Claims

Last time I saw her, Grandmother
had grown seamed as a Bedouin tent.
She had claimed the right
to sleep alone, to own
her nights, to never bear
the weight of sex again nor to accept
its gift of comfort, for the luxury
of stretching her bones.
She'd carried eight children,
three had sunk in her belly, *náufragos*
she called them, shipwrecked babies
drowned in her black waters.
Children are made in the night and
steal your days
for the rest of your life, amen. She said this
to each of her daughters in turn. Once she had made a
    pact
with man and nature and kept it. Now like the sea,
she is claiming back her territory.

JUDITH ORTIZ COFER

254

My Grandmother's Ghost

She skimmed the yellow water like a moth,
Trailing her feet across the shallow stream;
She saw the berries, paused and sampled them
Where a slight spider cleaned his narrow tooth.
Light in the air, she fluttered up the path,
So delicate to shun the leaves and damp,
Like some young wife, holding a slender lamp
To find her stray child, or the moon, or both.

Even before she reached the empty house,
She beat her wings ever so lightly, rose,
Followed a bee where apples blew like snow;
And then, forgetting what she wanted there,
Too full of blossom and green light to care,
She hurried to the ground, and slipped below.

JAMES WRIGHT

My Grandmother in Paris

Paris. 1900. A sky of corrugated iron. Snow and mud.
Beggars like heaps of debris on street corners.
Women with pink cheeks melting in doorways.
Splashes of laughter, church bells, creaking boots.
Puccini's Paris, Paris of *La Bohème*, Paris
of garrets and prisons, Paris of sweet fevers, Paris

of phlegm and sweat, ivory breasts, skylights, *opéra:*
Paris of Wagner and Rilke, Paris of delicious
nineteenth-century melancholy, Paris where streetlights
glisten through the winter twilight
like pomegranates in hell.
                              Twilight.

My grandmother walks in the Bois de Boulogne
under frosted chestnuts. She's twelve years old,
a roundfaced girl just come from Russia,
her hair in skinny braids
like strange embroidery around her head.
She's on her way to the house of the Russian priest

where her mother cooks and cleans
but she watches, wondering, as carriages plunge
through the slush of the Bois, their lamps
leaping like goblin heads, their blanketed horses
clopping docile as cows through all the Paris noise.
Baudelaire is dead, Rimbaud dead in Africa, Gertrude
    Stein

thinking in Baltimore, Picasso painting in Barcelona.
My grandmother has learned three words of French:
allo, comment, combien. Amedée, the boy she's

going to marry four years from now
is in Nice with his sister Eugénie,
who will die next year at nineteen,

and his sister Rosette, who will die at forty.
My grandmother is still tired from last week.
She stops to sit on a low wall beside the road
and begins to shape a tiny angel out of crumbs of snow.
From a passing *fiacre* a young clerk off to the *opéra*
sees her round pink face suspended like a small balloon

in the blue air.
                    What is she thinking
as she pats a cold celestial head and frozen wings?
Is she remembering the awful trainride
across Europe, the bonfires at the Polish border, the
        shouts
as the engine chuffed into Berlin? No. She rises,

makes her angel into a snowball and tosses it at a tree.
She's thinking of Russia, of her grandmother back in
        the room
in Rostov-on-the-Don, of the ice like silver on the river
all winter and long into spring, of the black fields
outside town and the old stories of Baba Yaga and the
        tales
she has also heard of the redhaired cossack

said to be her own father.
                    She walks faster.
It's late and cold. Her mother will worry.
The fat priest will be cross. Paris
grows around her like an enigmatic alphabet.
Even the trees are different here. No firs, no birches!

As she walks, Baba Yaga's house on chicken legs
steps delicately away across snowy meadows
and her father the cossack, with his furry animal head,
    fierce teeth, red beard,
gallops into glacial distances.
(Does she suspect that from now on
she'll never really know any language again?)

Tomorrow the priest will be sixty. To celebrate
he'll buy a Swiss cane at the Galéries Lafayette.

                                                    In

    seventy years
my grandmother will twirl that cane and dance a
    twostep
among the eucalyptuses above San Francisco Bay,
singing me the song about the lost princess of the
    Volga

while, far below, the cold Pacific
glitters like an ice field.

                                        SANDRA M. GILBERT

Birds on a Powerline

Mama Mary's counting them
Again. Eleven black. A single
Red one like a drop of blood

258

Against the sky. She's convinced
They've been there two weeks.
I bring her another cup of coffee

& a Fig Newton. I sit here reading
Frances Harper at the enamel table
Where I ate teacakes as a boy,

My head clear of voices brought back.
The green smell of the low land returns,
Stealing the taste of nitrate.

The deep-winter eyes of the birds
Shine in summer light like agate,
As if they could love the heart

Out of any wild thing. I stop,
With my finger on a word, listening.
They're on the powerline, a luminous

Message trailing a phantom
Goodyear blimp. I hear her say
Jesus, I promised you. Now

He's home safe, I'm ready.
My traveling shoes on. My teeth
In. I got on clean underwear.

YUSEF KOMUNYAKAA

One We Knew

(M.H. 1772–1857)

She told how they used to form for the country
    dances—
      "The Triumph," "The New-rigged Ship"—
To the light of the guttering wax in the panelled
    manses,
      And in cots to the blink of a dip.

She spoke of the wild "poussetting" and "allemanding"
    On carpet, on oak, and on sod;
And the two long rows of ladies and gentlemen
    standing,
      And the figures the couples trod.

She showed us the spot where the maypole was yearly
    planted,
      And where the bandsmen stood
While breeched and kerchiefed partners whirled, and
    panted
      To choose each other for good.

She told of that far-back day when they learnt
    astounded
      Of the death of the King of France:
Of the Terror; and then of Bonaparte's unbounded
    Ambition and arrogance.

Of how his threats woke warlike preparations
    Along the southern strand,
And how each night brought tremors and trepidations
    Lest morning should see him land.

She said she had often heard the gibbet creaking
    As it swayed in the lightning flash,
Had caught from the neighbouring town a small child's
        shrieking
    At the cart-tail under the lash. . . .

With cap-framed face and long gaze into the embers—
    We seated around her knees—
She would dwell on such dead themes, not as one who
        remembers,
    But rather as one who sees.

She seemed one left behind of a band gone distant
    So far that no tongue could hail:
Past things retold were to her as things existent,
    Things present but as a tale.

THOMAS HARDY

X

*A*FTER
MY MOTHER DIED:
PRAYERS AND
FAREWELLS

*I*t is often said that "the birth of children fore-
casts the death of parents," an adage that reminds us
how natural it is for children to outlive their mothers
and fathers. Still, the grief that accompanies the death of
a parent infuses the elegies collected in this section of
MotherSongs.

Of course enigmatic, incongruous aspects of death do
find expression as well. Robert Lowell's mother is
wrapped up like a sweet cake in a coffin with a mis-
spelled name; Molly Peacock's is buried with earrings
she couldn't stand wearing for more than two hours in
life; and Marilyn Hacker only fully comprehends the

reality of her mother's death at a fall sales counter in Macy's department store. But the realism of such accounts only emphasizes the point of these poetic works, most of which are motivated by just the stubborn refusal to accept death that Patrick Kavanagh expresses: "I do not think of you lying in the wet clay." Indeed, some of the greatest of these prayers and farewells counter the humiliations to which flesh is heir—aging, mental illness, physical deterioration—by bringing the mother at least imaginatively back to life through a kind of poetic resurrection.

From *Mourning Pictures*

Ladies and gentlemen, my mother is
dying. You say, "Everyone's mother dies."
I bow to you, smile. Ladies, gentlemen,
my mother is dying. She has cancer.
You say, "Many people die of cancer."
I scratch my head. Gentle ladies, gentle
men, my mother has cancer, and, short of
some miracle, will die. You say, "This has
happened many times before." You say, "Death
is something which repeats itself." I bow.
Ladies and gentlemen, my mother has cancer
all through her. She will die unless there's a
miracle. You shrug. You gave up religion
years ago. Marxism too. You don't believe
in anything. I step forward. My mother
is dying. I don't believe in miracles.
Ladies and gentlemen, one last time: My
mother's dying. I haven't got another.

HONOR MOORE

Sorrow

Why does the thin grey strand
Floating up from the forgotten

Cigarette between my fingers,
Why does it trouble me?

Ah, you will understand;
When I carried my mother downstairs,
A few times only, at the beginning
Of her soft-foot malady,

I should find, for a reprimand
To my gaiety, a few long grey hairs
On the breast of my coat; and one by one
I watched them float up the dark chimney.

D. H. LAWRENCE

The Bride

My love looks like a girl to-night,
        But she is old.
The plaits that lie along her pillow
        Are not gold,
But threaded with filigree silver,
        And uncanny cold.

She looks like a young maiden, since her brow
        Is smooth and fair;
Her cheeks are very smooth, her eyes are closed,

She sleeps a rare,
Still, winsome sleep, so still, and so composed.

Nay, but she sleeps like a bride, and dreams her
        dreams
                Of perfect things.
She lies at last, the darling, in the shape of her dream;
                And her dead mouth sings
By its shape, like thrushes in clear evenings.

D. H. LAWRENCE

Sailing Home from Rapallo

(February, 1954)

Your nurse could only speak Italian,
but after twenty minutes I could imagine your final
        week,
and tears ran down my cheeks. . . .
When I embarked from Italy with my Mother's body,
the whole shoreline of the *Golfo di Genova*
was breaking into fiery flower.
The crazy yellow and azure sea-sleds
blasting like jack-hammers across
the *spumante*-bubbling wake of our liner,
recalled the clashing colors of my Ford.
Mother travelled first-class in the hold;

her *Risorgimento* black and gold casket
was like Napoleon's at the *Invalides*. . . .

While the passengers were tanning
on the Mediterranean in deck-chairs,
our family cemetery in Dunbarton
lay under the White Mountains
in the sub-zero weather.
The graveyard's soil was changing to stone—
so many of its deaths had been midwinter.
Dour and dark against the blinding snowdrifts,
its black brook and fir trunks were as smooth as masts.
A fence of iron spear-hafts
black-bordered its mostly Colonial grave-slates.
The only "unhistoric" soul to come here
was Father, now buried beneath his recent
unweathered pink-veined slice of marble.
Even the Latin of his Lowell motto:
Occasionem cognosce,
seemed too businesslike and pushing here,
where the burning cold illuminated
the hewn inscriptions of Mother's relatives:
twenty or thirty Winslows and Starks.
Frost had given their names a diamond edge. . . .

In the grandiloquent lettering on Mother's coffin,
Lowell had been misspelled *LOVEL.*
The corpse
was wrapped like *panetone* in Italian tinfoil.

ROBERT LOWELL

A Woman Mourned by Daughters

Now, not a tear begun,
we sit here in your kitchen,
spent, you see, already.
You are swollen till you strain
this house and the whole sky.
You, whom we so often
succeeded in ignoring!
You are puffed up in death
like a corpse pulled from the sea;
we groan beneath your weight.
And yet you were a leaf,
a straw blown on the bed,
you had long since become
crisp as a dead insect.
What is it, if not you,
that settles on us now
like satin you pulled down
over our bridal heads?
What rises in our throats
like food you prodded in?
Nothing could be enough.
You breathe upon us now
through solid assertions
of yourself: teaspoons, goblets,
seas of carpet, a forest
of old plants to be watered,
an old man in an adjoining
room to be touched and fed.

And all this universe
dares us to lay a finger
anywhere, save exactly
as you would wish it done.

ADRIENNE RICH

Autumn 1980

For Judith McDaniel

I spent the night after my mother died
in a farmhouse north of Saratoga Springs
belonging to a thirty-nine-year-old
professor with long, silvered wiry hair,
a lively girl's flushed cheeks and gemstone eyes.
I didn't know that she had died.
Two big bitches and a varying
heap of cats snoozed near a black wood stove
on a rag rug, while, on the spring-shot couch
we talked late over slow glasses of wine.
In the spare room near Saratoga Springs
was a high box bed. My mother died
that morning, of heart failure, finally.
Insulin shocks burned out her memory.
On the bed, a blue early-century
Texas Star, in a room white and blue
as my flannel pajamas. I'd have worn

the same, but smaller, ten years old at home.
Home was the Bronx, on Eastburn Avenue,
miles south of the hermetic not-quite-new
block where they'd sent this morning's ambulance.
Her nurse had telephoned. My coat was on,
my book-stuffed bag already on my back.
She said, "Your mother had another shock.
We'll be taking her to the hospital."
I asked if I should stay. She said, "It's all
right." I named the upstate college where
I'd speak that night. This had happened before.
I knew/I didn't know: it's not the same.
November cold was in that corner room
upstairs, with a frame window over land
the woman and another woman owned
—who was away. I thought of her alone
in her wide old bed, me in mine. I turned
the covers back. I didn't know she had died.
The tan dog chased cats; she had to be tied
in the front yard while I went along
on morning errands until, back in town,
I'd catch my bus. November hills were raw
fall after celebratory fall
foliage, reunions, festival.
I blew warmth on my hands in a dark barn
where two shaggy mares whuffled in straw,
dipped steaming velvet muzzles to the pail
of feed. We'd left the pickup's heater on.
It smelled like kapok when we climbed inside.
We both unzipped our parkas for the ride

back to the Saratoga bus station.
I blamed the wind if I felt something wrong.
A shrunken-souled old woman whom I saw
once a month lay on a hospital
slab in the Bronx. Mean or not, that soul
in its cortège of history was gone.
I didn't know that I could never know,
now, the daughtering magic to recall
across two coffee-mugs the clever Young
Socialist whose views would coincide
with mine. I didn't know that she had died.
Not talking much, while weighted sky pressed down,
we climbed the back road's bosom to the all-
night diner doubling as a bus depot.
I brushed my new friend's cool cheek with my own,
and caught the southbound bus from Montreal.
I counted boarded-up racetrack motel
after motel. I couldn't read. I tried
to sleep. I didn't know that she had died.
Hours later, outside Port Authority,
rained on, I zipped and hooded an obscure
ache from my right temple down my shoulder,
Anonymous in the mid-afternoon
crowds, I'd walk, to stretch, I thought, downtown.
I rode on the female wave, typically
into Macy's (where forty-five years
past, qualified by her new M.A.
in Chemistry, she'd sold Fine Lingerie),
to browse in Fall Sale bargains for my child,
aged six, size eight, hung brilliantly or piled

like autumn foliage I'd missed somehow,
and knew what I officially didn't know
and put the bright thing down, scalded with tears.

MARILYN HACKER

Upon a Lady that dyed in child-bed,
and left a daughter behind her

As Gilly flowers do but stay
To blow, and seed, and so away;
So you sweet Lady (sweet as May)
The gardens-glory liv'd a while,
To lend the world your scent and smile.

But when your own faire print was set
Once in a Virgin *Flosculet,*
(Sweet as your selfe, and newly blown)
To give that life, resign'd your own:
But so, as still the mothers power
Lives in the pretty Lady-flower.

ROBERT HERRICK

Upon a young mother of many children

Let all chaste Matrons, when they chance to see
My num'rous issue: Praise, and pitty me.
Praise me, for having such a fruitfull wombe;
Pity me too, who found so soone a Tomb.

ROBERT HERRICK

C.L.M.

In the dark womb where I began,
My mother's life made me a man.
Through all the months of human birth
Her beauty fed my common earth.
I cannot see, nor breathe, nor stir,
But through the death of some of her.

Down in the darkness of the grave
She cannot see the life she gave.
For all her love, she cannot tell
Whether I use it ill or well,
Nor knock at dusty doors to find
Her beauty dusty in the mind.

If the grave's gates could be undone,
She would not know her little son,

274

I am so grown.   If we should meet,
She would pass by me in the street,
Unless my soul's face let her see
My sense of what she did for me.

What have I done to keep in mind
My debt to her and womankind?
What woman's happier life repays
Her for those months of wretched days?
For all my mouthless body leeched
Ere Birth's releasing hell was reached?

What have I done, or tried, or said
In thanks to that dear woman dead?
Men triumph over women still,
Men trample women's rights at will,
And man's lust roves the world untamed . . .
O grave, keep shut lest I be shamed.

JOHN MASEFIELD

In Memory of My Mother

I do not think of you lying in the wet clay
Of a Monaghan graveyard; I see
You walking down a lane among the poplars
On your way to the station, or happily

Going to second Mass on a summer Sunday—
You meet me and you say:
"Don't forget to see about the cattle—"
Among your earthiest words the angels stray.

And I think of you walking along a headland
Of green oats in June,
So full of repose, so rich with life—
And I see us meeting at the end of a town

On a fair day by accident, after
The bargains are all made and we can walk
Together through the shops and stalls and markets
Free in the oriental streets of thought.

O you are not lying in the wet clay,
For it is a harvest evening now and we
Are piling up the ricks against the moonlight
And you smile up at us—eternally.

PATRICK KAVANAGH

From *On the Receipt of My Mother's Picture out of Norfolk*

The Gift of My Cousin Ann Bodham

Oh that those lips had language! Life has pass'd
With me but roughly since I heard thee last.
Those lips are thine—thy own sweet smiles I see,
The same that oft in childhood solaced me;
Voice only fails, else, how distinct they say,
"Grieve not, my child, chase all thy fears away!"
The meek intelligence of those dear eyes
(Blest be the art that can immortalize,
The art that baffles time's tyrannic claim
To quench it) here shines on me still the same.
    Faithful remembrancer of one so dear,
Oh welcome guest, though unexpected, here!
Who bidd'st me honour with an artless song,
Affectionate, a mother lost so long,
I will obey, not willingly alone,
But gladly, as the precept were her own;
And, while that face renews my filial grief,
Fancy shall weave a charm for my relief—
Shall steep me in Elysian reverie,
A momentary dream, that thou art she.
    My mother! when I learn'd that thou wast dead,
Say, wast thou conscious of the tears I shed?
Hover'd thy spirit o'er thy sorrowing son,
Wretch even then, life's journey just begun?
Perhaps thou gav'st me, though unseen, a kiss;

Perhaps a tear, if souls can weep in bliss—
Ah that maternal smile! it answers—Yes.
I heard the bell toll'd on thy burial day,
I saw the hearse that bore thee slow away,
And, turning from my nurs'ry window, drew
A long, long sigh, and wept a last adieu!
But was it such?—It was.—Where thou art gone
Adieus and farewells are a sound unknown.
May I but meet thee on that peaceful shore,
The parting sound shall pass my lips no more!
Thy maidens griev'd themselves at my concern,
Oft gave me promise of a quick return.
What ardently I wish'd, I long believ'd,
And, disappointed still, was still deceiv'd;
By disappointment every day beguil'd,
Dupe of *to-morrow* even from a child.
Thus many a sad to-morrow came and went,
Till, all my stock of infant sorrow spent,
I learn'd at last submission to my lot;
But, though I less deplor'd thee, ne'er forgot.

WILLIAM COWPER

Museum Out of Mind

Whatever it was I used to call you out loud
when I was twenty, ten, or less, I forget. Odd—
I shy from recalling the syllables of how

the golden age once spoke (say, as we talked non-stop
after school, or having our hair done, or as you
chose green peas pod by pod while I watched you
    shop).

Later, myself mother, I called you the motherdear
no child of mine would use—but one of the baby
humwords must have come first. And I am infant here

before your advanced degrees in death, seeking speech
in words of a tongue I am spelling out of you who
    could,
by the stars and letters of a map you'd make, teach

(Queens Hermes, alphabet giver) anyone to find
the essential simple, and to translate all
locations into constellations of the mind.

I talk to your absence. Daft. Grotesque. I begin
to see you as grotesque, yes a joke, a guess,
a grotesque of the grave I wept to leave you in.

Birds love dead trees. They like to strip a shred of bark,
tug at it, shake it, lunch on eggcase and insect,
and I go after you like that. Graves are

grounded in the mind though the cemetery keeps
grounds & groundplan, their care perpetual; yours is
in the sad best section, comical—we Stoics

are all comics—among Mafia and their daily,
like you, communicant women. A solitary,
motherdear, you loved the look of community

as, dogged in practise, you believed undaunted
and behaved, relentlessly, as you believed,
so that at times your present company haunts me

like a storm of comic joy. Into the eight-body
plot grandma bought and put grandpa at the bottom,
she went next old raceme dry tiger lily;

then her son and then your man; there you now lie
kept from your father and mother by a layer
of brother and lover   and also by

the costumes, wood bronze lead satin silk & wool,
you each wear. Now you, famous for the Saturday
museum-hauls of your New York, ignore the full

shelves of the Costume Museum Out of Mind
you have entered. Once your heels & skirtshapes looked to
Paris; now you notice none of the well-defined

custom samples, filed as fashion and history;
beaded dresses, bow ties, hard collars, French chalk,
corsets, false cuffs, union suits, hand embroideries,

and decades of dressed hair, an outgrown show of
    styles,
some rotted, some stained; yet in your choice place are
    stored
shapes & modes that amply record our tribal

grasp of the honor of family, the dignity
of ritual, the self of death. There is not much
nourishment in this but I beak it out. Better be

choking down images of the set greywebbed hair
cocoon your skull is wearing and the tumbled nest
of cowlick at your nape, than to grimace and bear

as I bear the packet I found in your drawer, kept
hidden for sixty years but kept: the lissome, fresh,
bright chestnut yard of hair you cut

to enter the nineteen twenties. Dismay, dismay,
disgusting, it's beautiful, funny, it's yours, mama,
still in tissue paper, boxed, as I throw it away.

MARIE PONSOT

The Fare

Bury me in my pink pantsuit, you said—and I did.
But I'd never dressed you before! I saw the glint
of gold in your jewelry drawer and popped
the earrings in a plastic bag along with pearls,
a pink and gold pin, and your perfume. ("What's this?"
the mortician said . . . "Oh well, we'll spray some on.")
Now your words from the coffin: *Take my earrings off!*
I've had them on all day, for God's sake!
You've had them on five days. The lid's closed,
and the sharp stab of a femininity
you couldn't stand for more than two hours in life
is eternal—you'll never relax. I'm 400 miles away.
Should I call up the funeral home and have them
        removed?
You're not buried yet—stored till the ground thaws—
where, I didn't ask. Probably the mortician's garage.
I should have buried you in slippers and a bathrobe.
Instead, I gave them your shoes. Oh, please
do it for me. I can't stand the thought of you
pained by vanity forever. Reach your cold hand
up to your ear and pull and hear the click
of the clasp hinge unclasping, then reach
across your face and get the other one
and—this effort could take you days, I know,
since you're dead. Let it be your last effort:
to change my mistake and be dead in comfort.
Lower your hands in their places

on your low mound of stomach and rest, rest,
you can let go. They'll fall
to the bottom of the casket like tokens,
return fare fallen to the pit
of a coat's satin pocket.

MOLLY PEACOCK

Elegy for My Mother

She heard the least footfall, the least sigh
Or whisper beyond a door, the turning
Of a page in a far room, the most distant birdsong,

Even a slight wind when it was barely
Beginning; she would wait at a window
For someone to come home, for someone sleeping

To stir and waken, for someone far away
To tell her anything she could murmur
Word for word for years, for those close by

To be alive and well in stories she loved
To listen to all day, where life after life
Kept happening to others, but not to her,

And it was no surprise to forget herself
One morning, to misplace wherever she was,
Whoever she was, and become a ghostly wonder

Who would never wonder why it didn't matter
If no one listened to her or whether
She was here or there or even somewhere

Or why it felt so easy not to linger
In the doorway saying hello, goodbye, or remember
Me, but simply to turn and disappear.

DAVID WAGONER

Kaddish

Mother of my birth, for how long were we together
in your love and my adoration of your self?
For the shadow of a moment as I breathed your pain
and you breathed my suffering, as we knew
of shadows in lit rooms that would swallow the light.

Your face beneath the oxygen tent was alive
but your eyes were closed. Your breathing was hoarse
but your sleep was with death. I was alone with you
as it was when I was young but only alone now
and now with you. I was to be alone forever
as I was learning, watching you become alone.

Earth is your mother as you were mine, my earth,
my sustenance, my comfort and my strength

and now without you I turn to your mother
and seek from her that I may meet you again
in rock and stone: whisper to the stone,
I love you; whisper to the rock, I found you;
whisper to earth, Mother, I have found my mother
and I am safe and always have been.

DAVID IGNATOW

XI

THE MOTHER OF US ALL: MYTHS OF MATERNITY

$\mathcal{F}$or some who were brought up in a religion dedicated to God the Father it may come as a surprise to learn that most cultures, including our own, originally worshiped mother goddesses. Even Sigmund Freud was bemused by this phenomenon, rather nervously confessing in *Totem and Taboo* that "I am at a loss to indicate the place of the great maternal deities who perhaps everywhere preceded the paternal deities." Yet although anthropologists only began to study matriarchal theology in the nineteenth century, from ancient times to the present poets have always praised the Great Mother and always celebrated what the dancer Isadora Duncan once called "the Mother Cry of all Creation."

Hera, Juno, Kali, Eve, Mary, Demeter, Gaia, Spider

Woman, Anansi: the goddess has many names, many faces, many moods. She is Mother Nature and Mother Earth, Madonna of Heaven and Star of the Sea. Sometimes deadly, she threatens to devour or destroy her children; often nurturing or inspiring, she is muse and mistress who makes poetry possible.

A number of the writers whose works we have included in this section identify the goddess with nature (Whitman, Dickinson) or with primordial *human* nature (Snyder). Others explore her classical incarnations, seriously or comically dramatizing her role as the deadly Medea (Wakoski), the powerful Demeter (Raine), or the fertile Maia (Keats). At the same time, in poems about Eve and Mary, many investigate and celebrate her importance to Judeo-Christian theology.

Is the true goddess "a bearded queen, wicked in her dead light," as Wallace Stevens claims of his sinister "Madame La Fleurie," or is she the tender "Mother of All" whom Whitman encounters in a vision? Is she Kali or Mary? Perhaps there is no single way of defining her, but all our poets would agree with the medieval bard who declared that "I sing of a maiden/That is makeless" [matchless], an incomparable, often incomprehensible yet always glamorous figure.

For a Fifty-Year-Old Woman
in Stockholm

Your firm chin
  straight brow
    tilt of the head

Knees up in an easy squat
    your body shows how
You gave birth nine times:
The dent in the bones
        in the back of the pelvis
    mother of us all,
        four thousand years dead.

GARY SNYDER

The White Goddess

All saints revile her, and all sober men
Ruled by the God Apollo's golden mean—
In scorn of which we sailed to find her
In distant regions likeliest to hold her
Whom we desired above all things to know,
Sister of the mirage and echo.

It was a virtue not to stay,
To go our headstrong and heroic way
Seeking her out at the volcano's head,
Among pack ice, or where the track had faded
Beyond the cavern of the seven sleepers:
Whose broad high brow was white as any leper's,
Whose eyes were blue, with rowan-berry lips,
With hair curled honey-coloured to white hips.

Green sap of Spring in the young wood a-stir
Will celebrate the Mountain Mother,
And every song-bird shout awhile for her;
But we are gifted, even in November
Rawest of seasons, with so huge a sense
Of her nakedly worn magnificence
We forget cruelty and past betrayal,
Heedless of where the next bright bolt may fall.

ROBERT GRAVES

In the Carolinas

The lilacs wither in the Carolinas.
Already the butterflies flutter above the cabins.
Already the new-born children interpret love
In the voices of mothers.

Timeless mother,
How is it that your aspic nipples
For once vent honey?

The pine-tree sweetens my body
The white iris beautifies me.

WALLACE STEVENS

Sweet Mountains—Ye tell Me no lie—

Sweet Mountains—Ye tell Me no lie—
Never deny Me—Never fly—
Those same unvarying Eyes
Turn on Me—when I fail—or feign,
Or take the Royal names in vain—
Their far—slow—Violet Gaze—

My Strong Madonnas—Cherish still—
The Wayward Nun—beneath the Hill—
Whose service—is to You—
Her latest Worship—When the Day
Fades from the Firmament away—
To lift Her Brows on You—

EMILY DICKINSON

The Earthwoman and the Waterwoman

The earthwoman by her oven
        tends her cakes of good grain.
The waterwoman's children
are spindle thin.
                The earthwoman
        has oaktree arms. Her children
full of blood and milk
        stamp through the woods shouting.
                The waterwoman
        sings gay songs in a sad voice
                with her moonshine children.
When the earthwoman
has had her fill of the good day
        she curls to sleep in her warm hut
        a dark fruitcake sleep
but the waterwoman
                goes dancing in the misty lit-up town
        in dragonfly dresses and blue shoes.

DENISE LEVERTOV

Kore in Hades

I came, yes, dear, dear
Mother for you I came, so I remember,

To lie in your warm
Bed, to watch the wonder flame:
Burning, golden gentle and bright the light of the living

With you I ran
To see the roadside green
Leaves and small cool bindweed flowers
Living rejoicing to proclaim
We are, we are manifold, in multitude
We come, we are near and far,
Past and future innumerable, we are yours,
We are you. I listened
To the sweet bird whose song is for ever,
I was the little girl of the one mother.

World you wove me to please a child,
Yet its texture was thinner than light, fleeter
Than flame that burned while it seemed
Leaves and flowers and garden world without end.
Bright those faces closed and were over.

Here and now is over, the garden
Lost from time, its sun its moon
Mother, daughter, daughter, mother, never
Is now: there is nothing, nothing for ever.

KATHLEEN RAINE

Medea the Sorceress

She is in the Home for Unwed Mothers in
Pasadena, the only girl who reads poetry. He
writes to her from his prep school, and she memorizes
the sonnets of Shakespeare as she takes her exercise
on the dusty, scrubby grounds of
The Home.

No enchantment changes her life.
She is told by the Social Worker that she has
FAILED because
> she still loves J
> she doesn't regret doing anything for love,
> she doesn't believe she is bad
> she doesn't regret giving up her child
> she believes her life will go on, the same as it
>   has always gone on
> she won't talk about her mistakes.

This is the same as being on the desert,
this life in the linoleum-floored room,
eating with girls who have been raped by their fathers,
and girls who got caught but didn't know with what
    man
and girls who were only 13
and girls who were nurses sleeping with doctors
and girls who wanted to forget everything and join the
    army,
girls who were all pregnant and ashamed and who knew
    they were

wandering some desert, though most of them, most
of us, didn't know
the names of desert rattlers, or moths like the Dusty
    Silverwing, or
about the tiny burrowing owls, or the lingering scent of
    sagebrush
when the night was pure, pure as we knew we still were.

So, as if she were Medea, when the letters came
talking casually about his dates with other girls, un-
    pregnant girls,
she decided that she would have no choice. She
would kill him, and her children, and like the Sorceress
leave for another world, in her chariot drawn by
    dragons.

She gave up her baby. No regrets. Only the weak
have regrets.
She went to Berkeley, and she told him
to go away. No regrets. Only the weak have
regrets. She flew in her chariot
with all her dragonlady power to Berkeley,
then New York, then the Midwest, and finally to this
    Cafe
where she sits telling the tale, not of the tribe,
but of herself, and in spite of what others say, she
    knows
that the song this Silvery Moon Questing Lady of
    Dragonlight sings,
is the tale for at least half
of the tribe.

Strum, Gunslinger.
Hail, Maximus,
Ascent is descent, Dr. Paterson,
O, Love, one-eyed poet, where are you leading me now.
    No one should
be at the Home for Unwed Mothers. That is the real
    Wasteland.
These epistles, not Cantos or songs will be for Craig,
    Knight of
Hummingbird Light,
for Jonathan who understands the myth of the woman
    "Sleeping In
Flame,"
for Steel Man, my husband, who loves me at night in
    his invisible Cap of
Darkness,
and for all women, the other half of the tribe,
for Eve who dared to eat the apple,
I write this letter, and sign myself
Diane,

The Lady of Light.

DIANE WAKOSKI

Fragment of an Ode to Maia

Mother of Hermes! and still youthful Maia!
       May I sing to thee
As thou wast hymned on the shores of Baiæ?
       Or may I woo thee
In earlier Sicilian? or thy smiles
Seek as they once were sought, in Grecian isles,
By bards who died content on pleasant sward,
   Leaving great verse unto a little clan?
O, give me their vigour, and unheard
   Save of the quiet primrose, and the span
       Of heaven and few ears,
Rounded by thee, my song should die away
       Content as theirs,
Rich in the simple worship of a day.

JOHN KEATS

From *My Sisters, O My Sisters*

Eve and Mary the mother are our stem;
All our centuries go back to them.
And delicate the balance lies
Between the passionate and wise:
Of man's rib, one, and cleaves to him;
And one bears man and then frees him.
This double river has created us,
Always the rediscovered, always the cherished.
(But many fail in this. Many have perished.)

Hell is the loss of balance when woman is destroyer.
Each of us has been there.
Each of us knows what the floods can do.
How many women mother their husbands
Out of all strength and secret *Virtu;*
How many women love an only son
As a lover loves, binding the free hands.
How many yield up their true power
Out of weakness, the moment of passion
Betrayed by years of confused living—
For it is surely a lifetime work,
This learning to be a woman.
Until at the end what is clear
Is the marvelous skill to make
Life grow in all its forms.

Is knowing where to ask, where to yield,
Where to sow, where to plough the field,

Where to kill the heart or let it live;
To be Eve, the giver of knowledge, the lover;
To be Mary, the shield, the healer and the mother.
The balance is eternal whatever we may wish;
The law can be broken but we cannot change
What is supremely beautiful and strange.
Where find the root? Where re-join the source?
The fertile feminine goddess, double river?

MAY SARTON

Eve to Her Daughters

It was not I who began it.
Turned out into draughty caves,
hungry so often, having to work for our bread,
hearing the children whining,
I was nevertheless not unhappy.
Where Adam went I was fairly contented to go.
I adapted myself to the punishment: it was my life.

But Adam, you know . . . !
He kept on brooding over the insult,
over the trick They had played on us, over the scolding.

He had discovered a flaw in himself
and he had to make up for it.

Outside Eden the earth was imperfect,
the seasons changed, the game was fleet-footed,
he had to work for our living, and he didn't like it.
He even complained of my cooking
(it was hard to compete with Heaven).

So he set to work.
The earth must be made a new Eden
with central heating, domesticated animals,
mechanical harvesters, combustion engines,
escalators, refrigerators,
and modern means of communication
and multiplied opportunities for safe investment
and higher education for Abel and Cain
and the rest of the family.
You can see how his pride had been hurt.

In the process he had to unravel everything,
because he believed that mechanism
was the whole secret—he was always mechanical-
        minded.
He got to the very inside of the whole machine
exclaiming as he went, So this is how it works!
And now that I know how it works, why, I must have
        invented it.
As for God and the Other, they cannot be
        demonstrated,

and what cannot be demonstrated
doesn't exist.
You see, he had always been jealous.

Yes, he got to the centre
where nothing at all can be demonstrated.
And clearly he doesn't exist; but he refuses
to accept the conclusion.
You see, he was always an egotist.

It was warmer than this in the cave;
there was none of this fall-out.
I would suggest, for the sake of the children,
that it's time you took over.

But you are my daughters, you inherit my own faults of
        character;
you all are submissive, following Adam
even often beyond existence.
Faults of character have their own logic
and it always works out.
I observed this with Abel and Cain.

Perhaps the whole elaborate fable
right from the beginning
is meant to demonstrate this; perhaps it's the whole
        secret.
Perhaps nothing exists but our faults?
At least they can be demonstrated.

But it's useless to make
such a suggestion to Adam.
He has turned himself into God,
Who is faultless, and doesn't exist.

JUDITH WRIGHT

the astrologer predicts at mary's birth

this one lie down on grass.
this one old men will follow
calling mother   mother.
she womb will blossom then die.
this one she hide from evening.
at a certain time when she hear something
it will burn her ear.
at a certain place when she see something
it will break her eye.

LUCILLE CLIFTON

I Sing of a Maiden

I sing of a maiden
    That is makelees:
King of alle kinges
    To her sone she chees.

He cam also stille
    Ther his moder was
As dewe in Aprille
    That falleth on the gras.

He cam also stille
    To his modres bowr
As dewe in Aprille
    That falleth on the flowr.

He cam also stille
    Ther his moder lay
As dewe in Aprille
    That falleth on the spray.

Moder and maiden
    Was nevere noon but she:
Wel may swich a lady
    Godes moder be.

ANONYMOUS

ANA$\begin{bmatrix} \text{MARY} \\ \text{ARMY} \end{bmatrix}$GRAM

How well her name an "Army" doth present,
In whom the "Lord of Hosts" did pitch His tent!

GEORGE HERBERT

On the Blessed Virgins bashfulnesse

That on her lap she casts her humble Eye;
'Tis the sweet pride of her Humility.
The faire starre is well fixt, for where, ô where
Could she have fixt it on a fairer Spheare?
'Tis Heav'n 'tis Heaven she sees, Heavens God there
    lyes
She can see heaven, and ne're lift up her eyes:
This new Guest to her Eyes new Lawes hath given,
'Twas once *looke up,* 'tis now *looke downe* to Heaven.

RICHARD CRASHAW

Annunciation

Salvation to all that will is nigh,
That All, which alwayes is All every where,
Which cannot sinne, and yet all sinnes must beare,
Which cannot die, yet cannot chuse but die,
Loe, faithfull Virgin, yeelds himself to lye
In prison, in thy wombe; and though he there
Can take no sinne, nor thou give, yet he'will weare
Taken from thence, flesh, which deaths force may trie.
Ere by the spheares time was created, thou
Wast in his minde, who is thy Sonne, and Brother,
Whom thou conceiv'st, conceiv'd; yea thou art now
Thy Makers maker, and thy Fathers mother,
Thou'hast light in darke; and shutst in little roome,
Immensity cloysterd in thy deare wombe.

JOHN DONNE

Nativitie

Immensitie cloysterd in thy deare wombe,
Now leaves his welbelov'd imprisonment,
There he hath made himselfe to his intent
Weake enough, now into our world to come;
But Oh, for thee, for him, hath th' Inne no roome?
Yet lay him in this stall, and from the Orient,

Starres, and wisemen will travell to prevent
Th'effect of *Herods* jealous generall doome;
Seest thou, my Soule, with thy faiths eyes, how he
Which fils all place, yet none holds him, doth lye?
Was not his pity towards thee wondrous high,
That would have need to be pittied by thee?
Kisse him, and with him into Egypt goe,
With his kinde mother, who partakes thy woe.

JOHN DONNE

The Virgin Mary

For that faire blessed Mother-maid,
Whose flesh redeem'd us; That she-Cherubin,
    Which unlock'd Paradise, and made
One claime for innocence, and disseiz'd sinne,
        Whose wombe was a strange heav'n for there
        God cloath'd himselfe, and grew,
Our zealous thankes wee poure. As her deeds were
Our helpes, so are her prayers; nor can she sue
In vaine, who hath such title unto you.

JOHN DONNE

The Mother of God

The threefold terror of love; a fallen flare
Through the hollow of an ear;
Wings beating about the room;
The terror of all terrors that I bore
The Heavens in my womb.

Had I not found content among the shows
Every common woman knows,
Chimney corner, garden walk,
Or rocky cistern where we tread the clothes
And gather all the talk?

What is this flesh I purchased with my pains,
This fallen star my milk sustains,
This love that makes my heart's blood stop
Or strikes a sudden chill into my bones
And bids my hair stand up?

WILLIAM BUTLER YEATS

Observation

The Virgin-Mother stood at distance (there)
From her Sonnes Crosse, not shedding once a teare:
Because the Law forbad to sit and crie
For those, who did as malefactors die.
So she, to keep her mighty woes in awe,
Tortur'd her love, not to transgresse the Law.
Observe we may, how *Mary Joses* then,
And th'other *Mary* (*Mary Magdalen*)
Sate by the Grave; and sadly sitting there,
Shed for their Master many a bitter teare:
But 'twas not till their *dearest* Lord was dead;
And then to weep they both were licensed.

ROBERT HERRICK

The Virgin Mary

To work a *wonder*, God would have her shown,
At once, a Bud, and yet a *Rose full-blowne.*

ROBERT HERRICK

Another

As Sun-beames pierce the glasse, and streaming in,
No crack or Schisme leave i'th subtill skin:
So the Divine Hand work't, and brake no thred,
But, in a *Mother*, kept a *maiden-head.*

ROBERT HERRICK

Madame La Fleurie

Weight him down, O side-stars, with the great
    weightings of the end.
Seal him there. He looked in a glass of the earth and
    thought he lived in it.
Now, he brings all that he saw into the earth, to the
    waiting parent.
His crisp knowledge is devoured by her, beneath a dew.

Weight him, weight, weight him with the sleepiness of
    the moon.
It was only a glass because he looked in it. It was
    nothing he could be told.
It was a language he spoke, because he must, yet did not
    know.
It was a page he had found in the handbook of
    heartbreak.

The black fugatos are strumming the blacknesses of
  black . . .
The thick strings stutter the finial gutturals.
He does not lie there remembering the blue-jay, say the
  jay.
His grief is that his mother should feed on him, himself
  and what he saw,
In that distant chamber, a bearded queen, wicked in her
  dead light.

WALLACE STEVENS

My Mother Would Be a Falconress

My mother would be a falconress,
And I, her gay falcon treading her wrist,
would fly to bring back
from the blue of the sky to her, bleeding, a prize,
where I dream in my little hood with many bells
jangling when I'd turn my head.

My mother would be a falconress,
and she sends me as far as her will goes.
She lets me ride to the end of her curb
where I fall back in anguish.
I dread that she will cast me away,
for I fall, I mis-take, I fail in her mission.

She would bring down the little birds.
And I would bring down the little birds.
When will she let me bring down the little birds,
pierced from their flight with their necks broken,
their heads like flowers limp from the stem?

I tread my mother's wrist and would draw blood.
Behind the little hood my eyes are hooded.
I have gone back into my hooded silence,
talking to myself and dropping off to sleep.

For she has muffled my dreams in the hood she has
        made me,
sewn round with bells, jangling when I move.
She rides with her little falcon upon her wrist.
She uses a barb that brings me to cower.
She sends me abroad to try my wings
and I come back to her. I would bring down
the little birds to her
I may not tear into, I must bring back perfectly.

I tear at her wrist with my beak to draw blood,
and her eye holds me, anguisht, terrifying.
She draws a limit to my flight.
Never beyond my sight, she says.

She trains me to fetch and to limit myself in fetching.
She rewards me with meat for my dinner.
But I must never eat what she sends me to bring her.

Yet it would have been beautiful, if she would have
    carried me,
always, in a little hood with the bells ringing,
at her wrist, and her riding
to the great falcon hunt, and me
flying up to the curb of my heart from her heart
to bring down the skylark from the blue to her feet,
straining, and then released for the flight.

My mother would be a falconress,
and I her gerfalcon, raised at her will,
from her wrist sent flying, as if I were her own
pride, as if her pride
knew no limits, as if her mind
sought in me flight beyond the horizon.

Ah, but high, high in the air I flew.
And far, far beyond the curb of her will,
were the blue hills where the falcons nest.
And then I saw west to the dying sun—
it seemed my human soul went down in flames.

I tore at her wrist, at the hold she had for me,
until the blood ran hot and I heard her cry out,
far, far beyond the curb of her will

to horizons of stars beyond the ringing hills of the
    world where the falcons nest
I saw, and I tore at her wrist with my savage beak.
I flew, as if sight flew from the anguish in her eye
    beyond her sight,

sent from my striking loose, from the cruel strike at her
    wrist,
striking out from the blood to be free of her.

My mother would be a falconress,
and even now, years after this,
when the wounds I left her had surely heald,
and the woman is dead,
her fierce eyes closed, and if her heart
were broken, it is stilld

I would be a falcon and go free.
I tread her wrist and wear the hood,
talking to myself, and would draw blood.

ROBERT DUNCAN

Pensive on Her Dead Gazing

Pensive on her dead gazing I heard the Mother of All,
Desperate on the torn bodies, on the forms covering the
    battle-fields gazing,
(As the last gun ceased, but the scent of the powder-
    smoke linger'd,)
As she call'd to her earth with mournful voice while she
    stalk'd,
Absorb them well O my earth, she cried, I charge you
    lose not my sons, lose not an atom,
And you streams absorb them well, taking their dear
    blood,
And you local spots, and you airs that swim above
    lightly impalpable,
And all you essences of soil and growth, and you my
    rivers' depths,
And you mountain sides, and the woods where my dear
    children's blood trickling redden'd,
And you trees down in your roots to bequeath to all
    future trees,
My dead absorb or South or North—my young men's
    bodies absorb, and their precious precious blood,
Which holding in trust for me faithfully back again
    give me many a year hence,
In unseen essence and odor of surface and grass,
    centuries hence,
In blowing airs from the fields back again give me my
    darlings, give my immortal heroes,

Exhale me them centuries hence, breathe me their
    breath, let not an atom be lost,

O years and graves! O air and soil! O my dead, an
    aroma sweet!
Exhale them perennial sweet death, years, centuries
    hence.

                              WALT WHITMAN

XII

CONCEIVING THE MOTHER: MEANINGS OF MATERNITY

*W*hat does it mean—morally, politically, metaphysically—to be a mother? What does it mean—philosophically—to have or to have had a mother? On a primary level, of course, being and having a mother means being part of the biological world, part of what thinkers used to call "the great chain of being" that links the simplest cell with the most complex organism. Yet as the poems in this section about nonhuman mothers suggest, even the most rudimentary procreativity can be said to have moral meanings. D. H. Lawrence's kangaroo seems to the poet to watch "with insatiable wistfulness," seems indeed to have spent "untold centuries" waiting for "a new signal from life." Ted Hughes imagines his lambs are crying "Mother Mother Mother" and "the mothers are crying./Nothing can resist that probe, that cry." Nurturing a brood of eggs, Marianne Moore's paper nautilus appears to understand that "love/is the only fortress/strong enough to trust to."

Even maternal love is not always a fortress, however, and the hand that rocks the cradle doesn't always rule the world, or so some writers argue here. "Children do not always mean/hope," notes Margaret Atwood, adding that "to some they mean despair." For Wordsworth, "Blessed is the infant babe," but Alice Meynell mourns that in wartime "she who slays is she who bears," because she bears children into an unbearable universe of death.

Perhaps inevitably, the meanings of motherhood are as mysteriously multiple and contradictory as the meanings of life itself. If it is ultimately through maternity that we are borne toward the distant future in what Maxine Kumin calls "the Envelope of Almost-Infinity," what is the end toward which and for which our mothers carried us and we must carry our children? In one of Ted Hughes's poems, the womb conceives the new yet is inconceivable in its purposes: paradoxically sad and sweet, blossoming and lamenting, the organ of motherhood "ponders/In its dark tree."

Unfolded out of the Folds

Unfolded out of the folds of the woman man comes
    unfolded, and is always to come unfolded,
Unfolded only out of the superbest woman of the earth
    is to come the superbest man of the earth,
Unfolded out of the friendliest woman is to come the
    friendliest man,
Unfolded only out of the perfect body of a woman can
    a man be form'd of perfect body,
Unfolded only out of the inimitable poems of woman
    can come the poems of man, (only thence have my
    poems come;)
Unfolded out of the strong and arrogant woman I love,
    only thence can appear the strong and arrogant man
    I love,
Unfolded by brawny embraces from the well-muscled
    woman I love, only thence come the brawny
    embraces of the man,
Unfolded out of the folds of the woman's brain come
    all the folds of the man's brain, duly obedient,
Unfolded out of the justice of the woman all justice is
    unfolded,
Unfolded out of the sympathy of the woman is all
    sympathy;
A man is a great thing upon the earth and through
    eternity, but every jot of the greatness of man is
    unfolded out of woman;

First the man is shaped in the woman, he can then be
shaped in himself.

WALT WHITMAN

The Womb

Ponders
In its dark tree

Like a crucifix, still empty—
Dreaming rituals of moon religions.

Dream after fruitless dream
Stains the feet of that tree
With salty drops of pain.

Between the fullness of its root
And the emptiness of its arms

It swells
A bud of hunger.

It blooms
A splitting sweetness.

It sings, through its flower
A silent lament

For the dark world
Hanging on its dark tree.

TED HUGHES

Kangaroo

In the northern hemisphere
Life seems to leap at the air, or skim under the wind
Like stags on rocky ground, or pawing horses, or
    springy scut-tailed rabbits.

Or else rush horizontal to charge at the sky's horizon,
Like bulls or bisons or wild pigs.

Or slip like water slippery towards its ends,
As foxes, stoats, and wolves, and prairie dogs.

Only mice, and moles, and rats, and badgers, and
    beavers, and perhaps bears
Seem belly-plumbed to the earth's mid-navel.
Or frogs that when they leap come flop, and flop to the
    centre of the earth.

But the yellow antipodal Kangaroo, when she sits up,
Who can unseat her, like a liquid drop that is heavy,
    and just touches earth.

The downward drip
The down-urge.
So much denser than cold-blooded frogs.

Delicate mother Kangaroo
Sitting up there rabbit-wise, but huge, plumb-weighted,
And lifting her beautiful slender face, oh! so much more
    gently and finely lined than a rabbit's, or than a
    hare's,
Lifting her face to nibble at a round white peppermint
    drop, which she loves, sensitive mother Kangaroo.

Her sensitive, long, pure-bred face.
Her full antipodal eyes, so dark,
So big and quiet and remote, having watched so many
    empty dawns in silent Australia.

Her little loose hands, and drooping Victorian
    shoulders.
And then her great weight below the waist, her vast pale
    belly
With a thin young yellow little paw hanging out, and
    straggle of a long thin ear, like ribbon,
Like a funny trimming to the middle of her belly, thin
    little dangle of an immature paw, and one thin ear.

Her belly, her big haunches
And, in addition, the great muscular python-stretch of
    her tail.

There, she shan't have any more peppermint drops.
So she wistfully, sensitively sniffs the air, and then
    turns, goes off in slow sad leaps

On the long flat skis of her legs,
Steered and propelled by that steel-strong snake of a tail.

Stops again, half turns, inquisitive to look back.
While something stirs quickly in her belly, and a lean
    little face comes out, as from a window,

Peaked and a bit dismayed,
Only to disappear again quickly away from the sight of
    the world, to snuggle down in the warmth,
Leaving the trail of a different paw hanging out.

Still she watches with eternal, cocked wistfulness!
How full her eyes are, like the full, fathomless, shining
    eyes of an Australian black-boy
Who has been lost so many centuries on the margins of
    existence!

She watches with insatiable wistfulness.
Untold centuries of watching for something to come,
For a new signal from life, in that silent lost land of the
    South.

Where nothing bites but insects and snakes and the
    sun, small life.
Where no bull roared, no cow ever lowed, no stag cried,

no leopard screeched, no lion coughed, no dog
barked,
But all was silent save for parrots occasionally, in the
haunted blue bush.

Wistfully watching, with wonderful liquid eyes.
And all her weight, all her blood, dripping sack-wise
down towards the earth's centre,
And the live little-one taking in its paw at the door of
her belly.

Leap then, and come down on the line that draws to the
earth's deep, heavy centre.

D. H. LAWRENCE

Sheep

1

The sheep has stopped crying.
All morning in her wire-mesh compound
On the lawn, she has been crying
For her vanished lamb. Yesterday they came.
Then her lamb could stand, in a fashion,
And make some tiptoe cringing steps.
Now he has disappeared.
He was only half the proper size.

And his cry was wrong. It was not
A dry little hard bleat, a baby cry
Over a flat tongue, it was human,
It was a despairing human smooth Oh!
Like no lamb I ever heard. Its hind legs
Cowered in under its lumped spine,
Its feeble hips leaned toward
Its shoulders for support. Its stubby
White wool pyramid head, on a tottery neck,
Had sad and defeated eyes, pinched, pathetic,
Too small, and it cried all the time
Oh! Oh! staggering toward
Its alert, baffled, stamping, storming mother
Who feared our intentions. He was too weak
To find her teats, or to nuzzle up in under,
He hadn't the gumption. He was fully
Occupied just standing, then shuffling
Toward where she'd removed to. She knew
He wasn't right, she couldn't
Make him out. Then his rough-curl legs,
So stoutly built, and hooved
With quality tips,
Just got in the way, like a loose bundle
Of firewood he was cursed to manage,
Too heavy for him, lending sometimes
Some support, but no strength, no real help.
When we sat his mother on her tail, he mouthed
    her teat,
Slobbered a little, but after a minute
Lost aim and interest, his muzzle wandered,

He was managing a difficulty
Much more urgent and important. By evening
He could not stand. It was not
That he could not thrive, he was born
With everything but the will—
That can be deformed, just like a limb.
Death was more interesting to him.
Life could not get his attention.
So he died, with the yellow birth mucus
Still in his cardigan.
He did not survive a warm summer night.
Now his mother has started crying again.
The wind is oceanic in the elms
And the blossom is all set.

2

The mothers have come back
From the shearing, and behind the hedge
The woe of sheep is like a battlefield
In the evening, when the fighting is over,
And the cold begins, and the dew falls,
And bowed women move with water.
Mother Mother Mother the lambs
Are crying, and the mothers are crying.
Nothing can resist that probe, that cry
Of a lamb for its mother, or a ewe's crying
For its lamb. The lambs cannot find
Their mothers among those shorn strangers.
A half hour they have lamented,
Shaking their voices in desperation.

Bald brutal-voiced mothers braying out,
Flat-tongued lambs chopping off hopelessness.
Their hearts are in panic, their bodies
Are a mess of woe, woe they cry,
They mingle their trouble, a music
Of worse and worse distress, a worse entangling,
They hurry out little notes
With all their strength, cries searching this way and
    that.
The mothers force out sudden despair, blaaa!
On restless feet, with wild heads.

Their anguish goes on and on, in the June heat.
Only slowly their hurt dies, cry by cry,
As they fit themselves to what has happened.

TED HUGHES

bee mother

> to Èva Ráth Stricker
> *from a Hungarian dictionary*

MOTHER   —anya, méh

MÉH   —bee; womb, uterus
méhébe fogadni   —to conceive
méhallas   —hive, shed
méhanya   —uterus

méhbaj	—hysteria, fits of the mother
méhbefogadás	—conception
méhbeli	—uterine
méhcsipés	—sting of a bee
méhdüh	—uterine fury
méhgörcs	—spasms in hysteria
méhgörcsös	—hysterical
méhgyümölcs	—fruit of the womb
méhhas	—bee house, apiary
méhhüvely	—vagina
méhkirálynö	—queen bee
méhkosár	—bee hive
méhmagzat	—embryo, fetus
méhraj	—swarm of bees
méhrajzas	—swarming of bees
méhser	—metheglin
méhszáj	—mouth of the womb
méhnyésztés	—bee farming
méhtükör	—speculum
méhüszög	—false conception

in my mother's lost language
    it suddenly becomes clear
        the hive we are born into
                the bee hum
            of all languages
    we speak or will never hear

MEREDITH STRICKER

The Paper Nautilus

For authorities whose hopes
are shaped by mercenaries?
   Writers entrapped by
   teatime fame and by
commuters' comforts? Not for these
   the paper nautilus
   constructs her thin glass shell.

   Giving her perishable
souvenir of hope, a dull
   white outside and smooth-
   edged inner surface
glossy as the sea, the watchful
   maker of it guards it
   day and night; she scarcely

   eats until the eggs are hatched.
Buried eightfold in her eight
   arms, for she is in
   a sense a devil-
fish, her glass ram's-horn-cradled freight
   is hid but is not crushed;
   as Hercules, bitten

   by a crab loyal to the hydra,
was hindered to succeed,
   the intensively

watched eggs coming from
the shell free it when they are freed—
    leaving its wasp-nest flaws
    of white on white, and close-

laid Ionic chiton-folds
like the lines in the mane of
    a Parthenon horse,
    round which the arms had
wound themselves as if they knew love
    is the only fortress
    strong enough to trust to.

MARIANNE MOORE

Christmas Carols

Children do not always mean
hope. To some they mean despair.
This woman with her hair cut off
so she could not hang herself
threw herself from a rooftop, thirty
times raped & pregnant by the enemy
who did this to her. This one had her pelvis
broken by hammers so the child
could be extracted. Then she was thrown away,
useless, a ripped sack. This one
punctured herself with kitchen skewers

and bled to death on a greasy
oilcloth table, rather than bear
again and past the limit. There
is a limit, though who knows
when it may come? Nineteenth-century
ditches are littered with small wax corpses
dropped there in terror. A plane
swoops too low over the fox farm
and the mother eats her young. This too
is Nature. Think twice then
before you worship turned furrows, or pay
lip service to some full belly
or other, or single out one girl to play
the magic mother, in blue
& white, up on that pedestal,
perfect & intact, distinct
from those who aren't. Which means
everyone else. It's a matter
of food & available blood. If mother-
hood is sacred, put
your money where your mouth is. Only
then can you expect the coming
down to the wrecked & shimmering earth
of that miracle you sing
about, the day
when every child is a holy birth.

MARGARET ATWOOD

Parentage

"When Augustus Caesar legislated against the unmarried citizens of Rome, he declared them to be, in some sort, slayers of the people."

Ah no! not these!
These, who were childless, are not they who gave
So many dead unto the journeying wave,
The helpless nurslings of the cradling seas;
Not they who doomed by infallible decrees
Unnumbered man to the innumerable grave.

But those who slay
Are fathers. Theirs are armies. Death is theirs—
The death of innocences and despairs;
The dying of the golden and the grey.
The sentence, when these speak it, has no Nay.
And she who slays is she who bears, who bears.

ALICE MEYNELL

Solomon's Sword

Today, I walked down to the field
where they measure the wheat into sheaves
and saw the boy bending over his sickle
harvesting with the others,

only the half of him showing,
his legs disappearing in the waist-high grain.
Twelve years since the night I was delivered of him,

and I lay back on my bed,
my body still hurting where he had torn it.
He was given to me. I was told what to do.
After I nursed him and they left,
he fell asleep on my bosom, his breath
sweet from the little I could give him.
Under his weight I fell asleep
and dreamed my body was a huge stone wheel
turning against its adversaries,
laboring against the bodies
that worked so hard at pleasure
to rid themselves of pleasure.

When I woke, or dreamed that I woke
I turned and found
his little body lay beneath me like a stone,
he made no cry at all.
I took my breast and nursed him,
his mouth filling up, his mouth
that demanded nothing, and the milk started
spilling across his cheeks,
into his nostrils, his open eyes,

and I thought, why should I not
share this abundance
with the infant sleeping in the next room,

his mother asleep beside him,
—we three were alone in the house then.
The blade that had earlier worked on me
still lay on the moonlit table—

I carried him to her, he weighed no more
than he had when I earlier held him,
he was no heavier than hers—

and I replaced her baby with the dead one.
In his wisdom, Solomon
should have slain the infant;
it would have been fair to cut it in half
and deliver me from my grief
a second time. It would have been fair
to divide the grief equally,
now that one has more and one has less.

JANE SHORE

A Fable

Two women with
the same claim
came to the feet of
the wise king. Two women,
but only one baby.

The king knew
someone was lying.
What he said was
Let the child be
cut in half; that way
no one will go
empty-handed. He
drew his sword.
Then, of the two
women, one
renounced her share:
this was
the sign, the lesson.
Suppose
you saw your mother
torn between two daughters:
what could you do
to save her but be
willing to destroy
yourself—she would know
who was the rightful child,
the one who couldn't bear
to divide the mother.

LOUISE GLÜCK

What Your Mother Tells You Now

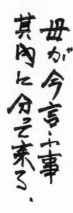

haha ga ima yu-koto
sono uchi ni
wakatte kuru

What your mother tells you
    now
in time
you will come to know.

MITSUYE YAMADA

The Envelope

It is true, Martin Heidegger, as you have written,
I fear to cease, even knowing that at the hour
of my death my daughters will absorb me, even
knowing they will carry me about forever
inside them, an arrested fetus, even as I carry
the ghost of my mother under my navel, a nervy
little androgynous person, a miracle
folded in lotus position.

Like those old pear-shaped Russian dolls that open
at the middle to reveal another and another, down

to the pea-sized, irreducible minim,
may we carry our mothers forth in our bellies.
May we, borne onward by our daughters, ride
in the Envelope of Almost-Infinity,
that chain letter good for the next twenty-five
thousand days of their lives.

MAXINE KUMIN

The Language of the Brag

I have wanted excellence in the knife-throw,
I have wanted to use my exceptionally strong and
     accurate arms
and my straight posture and quick electric muscles
to achieve something at the center of a crowd,
the blade piercing the bark deep,
the haft slowly and heavily vibrating like the cock.

I have wanted some epic use for my excellent body,
some heroism, some American achievement
beyond the ordinary for my extraordinary self,
magnetic and tensile, I have stood by the sandlot
and watched the boys play.

I have wanted courage, I have thought about fire
and the crossing of waterfalls, I have dragged around

my belly big with cowardice and safety,
my stool black with iron pills,
my huge breasts oozing mucus,
my legs swelling, my hands swelling,
my face swelling and darkening, my hair
falling out, my inner sex
stabbed again and again with terrible pain like a knife.
I have lain down.

I have lain down and sweated and shaken
and passed blood and feces and water and
slowly alone in the center of a circle I have
passed the new person out
and they have lifted the new person free of the act
and wiped the new person free of that
language of blood like praise all over the body.

I have done what you wanted to do, Walt Whitman,
Allen Ginsberg, I have done this thing,
I and the other women this exceptional
act with the exceptional heroic body,
this giving birth, this glistening verb,
and I am putting my proud American boast
right here with the others.

SHARON OLDS

Contributors' Notes

FLEUR ADCOCK, born in New Zealand, created several libretti for musical works by the composer Gillian Whitehead. Her *Selected Poems* was published in 1983.

AI, a native of Tucson, Arizona, has most recently published *Fate* (1991) and *Greed* (1993).

PAULA GUNN ALLEN is professor of Native American studies and ethnic studies at the University of California, Berkeley. In addition to a novel and critical works, she has published eight books of poetry, including *Skin and Bones: Poems 1979–87* (1988).

MARGARET ATWOOD, one of Canada's foremost writers, is famed for her essays, children's books, literary criticism, and poetry along with such novels as *Surfacing* (1972), *Lady Oracle* (1976), and *The Handmaid's Tale* (1986).

WENDY BARKER has published a critical study of Emily Dickinson as well as two collections of verse, most recently *Let the Ice Speak* (1992). She teaches at the University of Texas, San Antonio.

ANITA BARROWS has authored three collections of poetry, including *Emigration* (1972) and *The Limits* (1982).

JOHN BERRYMAN established his reputation with *Homage to Mistress Bradstreet* (1956), *77 Dream Songs,* (1964), and *His Toy, His Dream, His Rest* (1968).

ELIZABETH BISHOP was honored with numerous awards in her lifetime, including the Pulitzer Prize in 1955. She traveled extensively, and her sense of place influenced such collections as *North & South* (1946) and *Geography III* (1976).

WILLIAM BLAKE, the first of the great Romantic poets, remains best known for his *Songs of Innocence and of Experience* (1789) as well as his self-illustrated prophetic books, among them *The Marriage of Heaven and Hell* (1793) and *Jerusalem* (1820).

CHANA BLOCH, a professor of English at Mills College, is the author of two books of poetry as well as a critical study of George Herbert. Most recently, she has published a translation (with Ariel Bloch) of the biblical *Song of Songs* (1994).

EAVAN BOLAND is an Irish poet. Her most recent works are *Outside History, Selected Poems, 1980–1990* (1990), and *In a Time of Violence* (1994).

PEARL BOND is the author of *The Sensual Image* (1952).

ELIZABETH BOYD was an influential eighteenth-century poet, dramatist, and editor. Her best known works are the collection of poems *Variety* (1726) and the ballad-opera *Don Sancho, or The Student's Whim* (1739).

ANNE BRADSTREET was the author of *The Tenth Muse Lately Sprung Up in America* (1650), the first collection of verse to appear in the United States.

EMILY BRONTE's masterpiece, *Wuthering Heights,* appeared in 1847. Several years earlier, she and her sisters, Charlotte and Anne, had pseudonymously published *Poems by Currer, Ellis, and Acton Bell,* which sold two copies.

GWENDOLYN BROOKS has been Poet Laureate of Illinois and

the recipient of numerous awards, including the Pulitzer Prize. An activist leader in the civil rights movement, she has published more than thirteen volumes of poetry.

ELIZABETH BARRETT BROWNING was the foremost female poet of Victorian England. Still famed for her *Sonnets from the Portuguese*, she is increasingly well known for her verse novel, *Aurora Leigh*.

GLADYS CARDIFF is a Cherokee Indian who was born in Browning, Montana, where her parents were principal and music teacher on the Blackfoot reservation. She thinks of writing as "an act of affirmation and celebration."

LUCILLE CLIFTON is distinguished professor of humanities at St. Mary's College in Maryland. She is the author of seven books of poetry, including *The Book of Light* (1993) and numerous volumes of verse and fiction for children.

JUDITH ORTIZ COFER writes both prose and poetry. Her most recent publications are *Silent Dancing: A Partial Remembrance of a Puerto Rican Childhood* (1990) and a book of prose and poetry, *The Latin Deli* (1993).

ANITA SCOTT COLEMAN, who was born in Mexico and became a teacher, was a frequent contributor to *The Crisis* during the period called the Harlem Renaissance.

WANDA COLEMAN produced *Mad Dog Black Lady* in 1979 and her sixth book, *African Sleeping Sickness*, appeared in 1990.

JANE COOPER has taught at Sarah Lawrence College but currently dedicates herself full time to her writing. Her newest collection of poetry is *Green Notebook, Winter Road* (1994).

HART CRANE was an early twentieth-century American poet who died young. His major poem was *The Bridge* (1930).

RICHARD CRASHAW's devotional and metaphysical verse was heavily influenced by Italian, Spanish, and neo-Latin writings. His publications included *Sacred Epigrams* (1634) and *Carmen Deo Nostro* (1652).

E. E. CUMMINGS became famous for his unconventional typography and punctuation, producing such volumes as *Tulips and Chimneys* (1923), *XLI Poems* (1925), and *No Thanks* (1935).

LUCILLE DAY received the Joseph Henry Jackson Award for her book of poems *Self-Portrait with Hand Microscope* (1982). She lives in Berkeley, California, where she works as a math/science educational consultant.

EMILY DICKINSON, who published only eight poems before her death in 1886 and lived reclusively in Amherst, Massachusetts, is now considered one of America's greatest poets.

DIANE DI PRIMA is a widely published poet whose most recent works are *The Mysteries of Vision* (1988) and *Pieces of a Song* (1990).

JOHN DONNE wrote poems in a wide range of forms: satires, verse letters, marriage hymns, elegies, lyrics, and divine hymns. *Poems* (1635) was published four years after his death.

RITA DOVE, currently Poet Laureate of the United States, has authored many collections, including *Thomas and Beulah* (1986), which won the Pulitzer Prize for that year. She teaches at the University of Virginia.

ROBERT DUNCAN's work included verse dramas, translations, and nine books of poems; he spent most of his life in California. His last publication was *Ground Work II: In the Dark* (1987).

LYNN EMANUEL teaches at the University of Pittsburgh. Her most recent collections are *Hotel Fiesta* (1984) and *Dig* (1992).

KAREN FIZER was a teacher of philosophy who left the field in order to study poetics and write poetry. She is the author of *Words Like Fate and Pain* (1992).

CAROLYN FORCHÉ is the author of three books of poems, including *The Country Between Us*, a Lamont Poetry Selection in 1981. Her most recent book is *The Angel of History* (1994).

KATHLEEN FRASER is a poet and editor whose most recent book of poems is *Something (even human voices) in the foreground, a lake* (1989).

TESS GALLAGHER is a poet and short story writer; her most recent books are *Moon Crossing Bridge* (1992) and *Portable Kisses* (1992).

RICHARD GARCIA is a first-generation American and the author of a bilingual children's book, *My Otilia's Spirits.* His latest book of poems, *The Flying Garcias* (1993), was a Pitt Poetry Series selection.

CELIA GILBERT lives in Cambridge, Massachusetts. Her most recent book is *Bonfire* (1983).

SANDRA M. GILBERT's latest collection of poems is *Ghost Volcano* (1995). She teaches at the University of California, Davis, and has coauthored or coedited many works with Susan Gubar, including the *Norton Anthology of Literature by Women.*

LOUISE GLÜCK, a native New Yorker, has published many books of poetry. Her *The Wild Iris* (1992) won the Pulitzer Prize.

PATRICIA GOEDICKE is the author of nine books of poetry, of which the most recent is *Paul Bunyan's Bearskin* (1992). She teaches at the University of Montana.

ROBERT GRAVES was the author of 120 books of poetry, fiction, translation, and criticism; his best known works are *The White Goddess* (1947), a view of the poetic impulse, and the novel *I, Claudius* (1934).

MARILYN HACKER has received the National Book Award

and is the author of six books of poems, including the verse novel *Love, Death and the Changing of Seasons* (1986). Her most recent book is *Winter Numbers* (1994).

THOMAS HARDY is best known for such novels as *Jude the Obscure* (1895) and *Tess of the D'Urbervilles* (1891), but he also published much influential poetry, including *The Dynasts*, an ambitious long poem that appeared in 1927.

FRANCES E. W. HARPER was a black novelist, poet, lecturer, and reformer involved in the Abolitionist movement and Underground Railroad. Her volume of antislavery verse, *Poems on Miscellaneous Subjects* (1845), went through some twenty editions by 1874.

JUDITH HEMSCHMEYER teaches at the University of Central Florida, Orlando. Besides publishing several books of poetry, she has produced a translation of the complete poems of Anna Akhmatova.

GEORGE HERBERT's verse was collected in *The Temple* (1633), a volume that reflects the deeply religious character of his concerns as well as his interest in ingenious imagery.

ROBERT HERRICK, one of a group known as the Cavalier poets, published one large collection in 1648. *Hesperides* and *Noble Numbers* contain poems on secular and sacred subjects, respectively.

BRENDA HILLMAN, poet-in-residence at St. Mary's College, Moraga, and the recipient of many prizes, has most recently published *Bright Existence* (1993).

LANGSTON HUGHES, one of the major contributors to the Harlem Renaissance in the twenties and thirties, published *The Weary Blues* (1926), *Not Without Laughter* (1930), and *Montage of a Dream Deferred* (1951).

TED HUGHES became Poet Laureate of the United Kingdom after the publication of such works as *The Hawk in the Rain* (1957), *Lupercal* (1960), *Crow* (1970), and *Gaudete* (1977).

DAVID IGNATOW has published fifteen books of poetry and is the recipient of the Bollingen Award; his most recent book is *Against the Evidence* (1994).

GEORGIA DOUGLAS JOHNSON, playwright, feminist, and poet of the Harlem Renaissance, published four volumes of poetry, among them *Bronze* (1922).

JUDITH JOHNSON, a recipient of the Yale Younger Poets' Prize, is the author of seven books of poetry, of which the most recent is *The Ice Lizard* (1992). She teaches at the State University of New York at Albany.

ERICA JONG is a poet and novelist whose works include *Fear of Flying*. Her most recent book of poems is *Any Woman's Blues* (1990).

SHIRLEY KAUFMAN lives in Jerusalem and has written many books of poetry, including *Rivers of Salt* (1993).

PATRICK KAVANAGH was a well-known Irish poet. His works include *The Great Hunger* (1946) and *The Complete Poems* (1974), published six years after his death.

JOHN KEATS, a major Romantic poet, died tragically young. In 1819, his *annus mirabilis*, Keats produced his "great odes" and sonnets, for which he is most famous today.

RUDYARD KIPLING is best known for his poetry and fiction, such as the *Jungle Books* (1894, 1895) and *Kim* (1901), concerning the British colonial experience in India in the late nineteenth century.

CAROLYN KIZER received the Pulitzer Prize in Poetry in 1985. She is the author of seven books of poems, among them *Yin* (1984) and *Mermaids in the Basement* (1986).

IRENA KLEPFISZ is the author of four books of poetry and prose; her most recent verse collection is *A Few Words in the Mother Tongue* (1990).

YUSEF KOMUNYAKAA, who teaches at Indiana University, has published a number of volumes, including most recently

Neon Vernacular: New and Selected Poems (1993), for which he won both the Pulitzer and Tufts prizes.

MAXINE KUMIN lives in New Hampshire. The author of nine volumes of poetry, she received the Pulitzer Prize for *Up Country: Poems of New England: New and Selected Poems* (1974).

DORIANNE LAUX is the author of two books of poems: *Awake* (1990) and *What We Carry* (1994). She teaches at the University of Oregon.

D. H. LAWRENCE, innovative modern novelist and poet, was initially condemned by critics for producing "indecent" literature. Two of his major novels are *The Rainbow* (1915) and *Women in Love* (1920). Some of his finest poems appeared in *Birds, Beasts and Flowers* (1923).

URSULA K. LE GUIN is mainly known for such science fiction and fantasy novels as *The Left Hand of Darkness* (1969) and *The Dispossessed* (1974). *Always Coming Home* (1985), a multimedia work, includes poetry, illustration, and music.

DENISE LEVERTOV is the author of more than a dozen books of poems and two books of essays. Her most recent collection is *Evening Train* (1992).

PHILIP LEVINE is a winner of the National Book Award and the author of fourteen books of poems, including, most recently, *What Work Is* (1991).

LYN LIFSHIN is the author of many books of poems, including *Madonna Who Shifts for Herself* (1983) and *Not Made of Glass* (1987).

DOROTHY LIVESAY is a Canadian poet and lecturer whose poetry ranges in style from imagist (in *Green Pitcher* [1928]) to political (*Right Hand Left Hand* [1977]).

AUDRE LORDE was the author of numerous volumes of poetry, including *Cables to Rage* (1970), *Coal* (1976), and *Our Dead*

Behind Us (1986). She published four volumes of prose, among them *Zami: A New Spelling of My Name* (1982).

ROBERT LOWELL, one of the first of the "confessional poets," authored numerous volumes of poetry, including *Life Studies* (1959) and *For the Union Dead* (1964).

CYNTHIA MACDONALD, a psychoanalyst as well as a poet, founded the creative writing program at the University of Houston. Her most recent book of verse is *Living Wills: New and Selected Poems* (1991).

COLLEEN MCELROY, a professor of English at the University of Washington, Seattle, has published six books of poetry and two works of fiction. Her most recent volume of verse is *What Madness Brought Me Here: New and Selected Poems, 1968–1988* (1990).

PHYLLIS MCGINLEY published many volumes of humorous light verse in the thirties and forties as well as children's books and essays.

HEATHER MCHUGH, who has translated the poetry of Jean Follain and produced a book on aesthetics, recently collected her poetry in *Hinge and Sign: Poems, 1968–1993* (1994).

SANDRA MCPHERSON teaches at the University of California, Davis. Her most recent collections are *Streamers* (1988) and *The God of Indeterminacy* (1993).

JOHN MASEFIELD, author of *Saltwater Ballads* (1902) and the long poem *Everlasting Mercy*, was England's Poet Laureate from 1930 to 1967.

EDGAR LEE MASTERS gained fame with *Spoon River Anthology* (1915), free-verse epitaphs revealing the secret lives of people buried in a midwestern cemetery.

PAULA MEEHAN lives in Dublin, Ireland, where she has been the recipient of several arts awards. She is the author of three books of poems, most recently *The Man Who Was Marked by Winter* (1994).

JAMES MERRILL's shorter poems are collected in *From the First Nine, Poems 1946–1976* (1982). His most recent work includes *Late Settings* (1985) as well as several novels and a book of essays.

ALICE MEYNELL, journalist and feminist as well as essayist and poet, produced many successful volumes of poetry and essays. Admired by such authors as John Ruskin and William Rossetti, she was nominated for the Poet Laureateship in 1895.

EDNA ST. VINCENT MILLAY published plays and fiction in her lifetime in addition to twelve volumes of poetry. She received the Pulitzer Prize in 1924 for *The Harp-Weaver and Other Poems* (1923).

ALICE DUER MILLER, a popular American novelist and poet, worked for women's suffrage and published the satiric *Are Women People?* (1915). Her second "novel in verse," *The White Cliffs*, appeared in 1940.

HONOR MOORE, playwright and poet, has also edited an anthology, *The New Woman's Theatre* (1977). She is the author of a series of poems concerning her mother's death, which she later developed into a play entitled *Mourning Pictures.*

MARIANNE MOORE published thirteen volumes of poetry and won the Pulitzer Prize and the National Book Award for *Collected Poems* (1951).

CAROL MUSKE is the author of five books of poetry and fiction; the most recent are the novel *Dear Digby* (1989) and *Red Trousseau* (1993), a collection of poems. She teaches at the University of Southern California.

DIANA O'HEHIR writes both poetry and fiction and is the

author of two novels and three books of poems, the most recent of which is *Home Free* (1988). She is professor Emerita at Mills College.

SHARON OLDS teaches at New York University and at Goldwater Hospital. Her fourth and latest volume of verse is *The Father* (1993).

ALICIA OSTRIKER is a poet and critic whose works include literary criticism as well as eight books of poems, the most recent of which is *Green Age* (1993).

LINDA PASTAN, the author of eight volumes of poetry and the recipient of many awards, was appointed Poet Laureate of Maryland in 1991. Her most recent books are *Heroes in Disguise* (1991), and the forthcoming *An Early Afterlife* (1995).

MOLLY PEACOCK has been president of the Poetry Society of America and is the author of four books of poems, the most recent of which is *Original Love* (1995).

AMBROSE PHILIPS was a poet, playwright, and associate of the eighteenth-century essayists Addison and Steele.

KATHERINE PHILIPS, a seventeenth-century British poet, formed the center of an intellectual circle called the Society of Friendship. Known to her friends as the Matchless Orinda, she circulated many of her poems privately but published a few in her lifetime.

SYLVIA PLATH published her now classic novel *The Bell Jar* in 1963, but has remained most famous for the poems that appeared in *The Colossus* (1960) and *Ariel* (1965).

MARIE PONSOT lives in New York City and has been a professor at Queens College. Her collections include, most recently, *Admit Impediment* (1981) and *The Green Dark* (1988).

MINNIE BRUCE PRATT lives in New Jersey and won the Lamont Prize for her second volume, *Crime Against Nature* (1990).

KATHLEEN RAINE is a poet and critic whose works include *The Lion's Mouth* (1977), among other volumes of verse, as well as studies of various major poets.

BARBARA RAS edited *Costa Rica: A Traveler's Literary Companion* (1994). Her poems have appeared widely in various literary magazines. She is an editor at Sierra Club Books in San Francisco.

ADRIENNE RICH, activist and theorist as well as prizewinning poet and essayist, has become an influential voice in the women's movement today. *An Atlas of the Difficult World: Poems 1988–1991* (1991) is her most recent book of verse.

CHRISTINA ROSSETTI, a Victorian poet, is perhaps best known for her long poem, *Goblin Market.*

MURIEL RUKEYSER published eighteen volumes of poetry, a novel, and several critical studies. Her *Collected Poems* appeared in 1978.

MAY SARTON, novelist and poet, is also well known for such memoirs as *Journal of a Solitude* (1973) and *At Seventy* (1984).

ANNE SEXTON published eight volumes of poetry in her lifetime and won the Pulitzer Prize in 1966 for her third book, *Live or Die.*

KARL SHAPIRO, an essayist and novelist as well as a prolific poet, has been an editor and a professor. He won the Pulitzer Prize in 1945 for *V-Letter.*

JANE SHORE's most recent book, *The Minute Hand*, was the Lamont Poetry Selection in 1986. She teaches at George Washington University in Washington, D.C.

CHARLES SIMIC is a poet whose most recent publications are *The Book of Gods and Devils* (1990) and *Hotel Insomnia* (1992). He teaches at the University of New Hampshire.

STEVIE SMITH was the pseudonym of Florence Margaret

Smith. She authored several novels as well as more than ten collections of poetry, including her wry *Not Waving but Drowning* (1957).

GARY SNYDER was a member of the beat movement along with Allen Ginsberg and Jack Kerouac. He has written numerous volumes of poetry, including *Myths and Texts* (1960), and was awarded the Pulitzer Prize in 1975.

CATHY SONG's first book, *Picture Bride*, won the Yale Younger Poet's Prize. Her most recent collection is *Frameless Windows, Squares of Light* (1988). She lives in Honolulu.

ELIZABETH SPIRES's fourth collection of poetry, *Worlding* (1995), includes many poems centered on conception and childbirth. Her other books are *Globe* (1981), *Swan's Island* (1985), and *Annonciade* (1989). She lives in Baltimore with her husband and daughter.

WALLACE STEVENS, one of the most important poetic voices of the early twentieth century, worked as legal counsel for an insurance firm most of his life. At the same time, he wrote poetry that he published in various volumes and which was collected posthumously by his daughter, Holly Stevens, in *The Palm at the End of the Mind* (1967).

RUTH STONE, who teaches at SUNY, Binghamton, has published five volumes of poems, among them *Second Hand Coat* (1987) and *Who Is the Widow's Muse?* (1991). Her most recent collection is *Simplicity* (1995).

MEREDITH STRICKER is coeditor of *HOW(ever)* magazine. Her work has appeared in *Epoch, ink,* and the *New Hungarian Quarterly.*

GENEVIEVE TAGGARD was raised in Hawaii and educated at the University of California, Berkeley. She published a number of books of poems as well as a life of Emily Dickinson while teaching at Mount Holyoke, Bennington, and Sarah Lawrence. Her *Collected Poems* appeared in 1938.

SHARON THESEN, a Canadian poet and editor, has authored several books of poetry, including *The Pangs of Sunday* (1990).

DYLAN THOMAS was best known as a poet and reader of his own poetry, although he was also the author of autobiographical prose and a play. His last publication was *Collected Poems* (1953).

ALBERTA TURNER is a coeditor of *Field* and the author of *Lid and Spoon* (1976).

DAVID WAGONER is both a novelist and poet; he teaches at the University of Washington, Seattle. His most recent book of poems is *Through the Forest* (1987).

DIANE WAKOSKI, writer in residence and university distinguished professor at Michigan State University, has authored sixteen volumes of poetry, the most recent of which is *Medea the Sorceress* (1991).

ANNE WALDMAN, formerly assistant director of the Poetry Project at St. Mark's Church in the Bowery, New York City, has published *Helping the Dreamer: New and Selected Poems 1966–1988.*

ALICE WALKER is a poet and novelist whose novel *The Color Purple* won an American Book Award and the Pulitzer Prize. Her most recent verse collection is *Horses Make a Landscape Look More Beautiful* (1986).

JEANNE MURRAY WALKER is the author of *Fugitive Angels* (1985) and *Coming into History* (1990).

MARGARET WALKER is a prose writer as well as a poet. She has published five volumes of poetry but is also well known for her novel, *Jubilee* (1966).

RUTH WHITMAN is the author of eight books of poems; the most recent is *Hatshepshut, Speak to Me* (1992).

WALT WHITMAN, pioneering bard of nineteenth-century America, wrote and rewrote his masterpiece, *Leaves of Grass*, first published in 1855, throughout his lifetime.

C. K. WILLIAMS teaches at George Mason University and lives part of the time in Paris. He is the author of *A Dream of Mind* (1992) and *Flesh and Blood* (1987), for which he won the National Book Critics Circle prize.

WILLIAM CARLOS WILLIAMS, a New Jersey doctor, was one of the most innovative of the modernist poets. His verse ranges from compact imagist lyrics such as "The Red Wheelbarrow" to the ambitious book-length poem *Paterson* (1946–51).

ANNE WINTERS is the author of *The Key to the City* (1986) and translator of the poems of Robert Marteau.

NELLIE WONG, who lives in San Francisco, has published *Dreams in Harrison Railroad Park* (1983) and *The Death of Long Steam Lady* (1986). Her essay "In Search of the Self as Hero" deals with her identity as an Asian-American writer.

WILLIAM WORDSWORTH, one of England's greatest poets, outlined the aesthetic of the Romantic movement in his preface to *Lyrical Ballads* (1802).

C. D. WRIGHT has published numerous collections of poetry, among them *String Light* (1991). She teaches at Brown University.

JAMES WRIGHT produced many collections of verse, including *To a Blossoming Pear Tree* (1977). He taught at the University of Minnesota and Hunter College.

JUDITH WRIGHT, perhaps the best known Australian woman poet, has authored numerous volumes, including *Woman and Man* (1949).

WILLIAM BUTLER YEATS, one of Ireland's greatest writers,

was a man of the theater, an Irish Nationalist, and a mystic as well as a poet. He was awarded the Nobel Prize in 1927.

MITSUYE YAMADA teaches creative writing and is the founder of the Multicultural Women Writers Collective. She is the author of a volume of stories and a verse collection, *Camp Notes and Other Poems* (1976).

Credits

Fleur Adcock, "For Andrew" from *Selected Poems.* Copyright © 1967 by Oxford University Press. Reprinted with the permission of the publisher.

Ai, "The Expectant Father" from *Killing Floor.* Copyright © 1979 by Ai. Reprinted with the permission of Houghton Mifflin Company.

Paula Gunn Allen, "Grandmother" from *Coyote's Daylight Trip* (Albuquerque/Sante Fe: La Confluencia, 1976). Reprinted with the permission of the author and the author's agent, Diane Cleaver, Sanford J. Greenburger Associates.

Margaret Atwood, "Spelling" from *True Stories* (New York: Simon & Schuster, 1981). Copyright © 1981 by Margaret Atwood. Reprinted with the permission of the author. "Christmas Carols" from *Selected Poems II: Poems Selected and New 1976–1986.* Copyright © 1987 by Margaret Atwood. Reprinted with the permission of Houghton Mifflin Company.

Wendy Barker, "Identifying Things" from *Let the Ice Speak* (Greenfield Center, NY: Ithaca House Books/Greenfield Review Press, 1991). Copyright © 1991 by Wendy Barker. Reprinted with the permission of the author.

Anita Barrows, "Miscarriage." Reprinted with the permission of the author.

357

Index

371

374

376

378